Ireland

A nation, writes Mark O'Connell in his article in this volume, is a work of fiction, built on stories and sustained through acts of collective imagination. How else can we explain the divisive border that splits the island of Ireland – a border that since 1998, the key year of the Good Friday Agreement that brought peace to the island, has been invisible? The Republic of Ireland and Northern Ireland, which have been separate nations for only a century, came about as a result of narratives shaped on the other side of the Irish Sea, in Great Britain, the former colonial power that once again, with Brexit, seems to be upsetting the apple cart and reviving tensions that for years most people had believed consigned to history. A nation, however, is also a physical entity, its landscape: the jagged coastline that has allowed the Irish language to survive in isolated fishing communities – although for how much longer? – the unobstructed view across the ocean towards North America and inland across the green treeless hillsides. And then there are the post-industrial cities regenerated through a growing globalised economy and a net migration that has recently, for the first time in well over a century, turned positive. And at the centre, in the Midlands, the country's hidden core, its boglands, the peat from which – a particularly dirty form of fossil fuel – has been extracted to depletion, a symbol not only of independence and economic self-reliance but also of the challenges of the energy transition to come. And yet, as Colum McCann reminds us, a country is composed most of all of its people, in which case the future can only be bright, because the people of Ireland – those same people who marched *en masse* for peace in the 1990s – decided to take things into their own hands and determine for themselves what their nation should be. By finally breaking the cruel hold that the ultraconservative Catholic Church had over the Republic of Ireland they created their own democratic tools to change society from within, restoring to women the right to make decisions over their own bodies and opening up the institution of the family to all who want it, in the process freeing themselves from imposed narratives and proving once more that the Irish people are one step ahead of the politicians who represent them.

Contents

Kenneth O Halloran is a photographer based in Dublin. He was born in the west of Ireland and is a graduate of the Institute of Art, Design and Technology in Dún Laoghaire, Dublin, and holds a masters in fine art photography from the University of Ulster, Belfast. O Halloran's work has appeared in publications such as *The New York Times Magazine*, *The Sunday Times Magazine*, *Stern*, *Le Monde*, *Time*, *GEO*, the *FT Magazine* and *Cosmopolitan*. His work has been recognised by the Royal Hibernian Academy, American Photography, Alliance Française and the Taylor Wessing Photographic Portrait Prize. He is also a winner of a World Press Photo Award, the Terry O'Neill Photography Award and the Syngenta Photography Award. In 2017 he was shortlisted for the Hennessy Portrait Prize. He has exhibited in Dublin at the Irish Museum of Modern Art, the Royal Hibernian Academy and the National Gallery of Ireland, in London at the National Portrait Gallery and the Photographers' Gallery and at the Sirius Arts Centre in Cork and Void Derry.

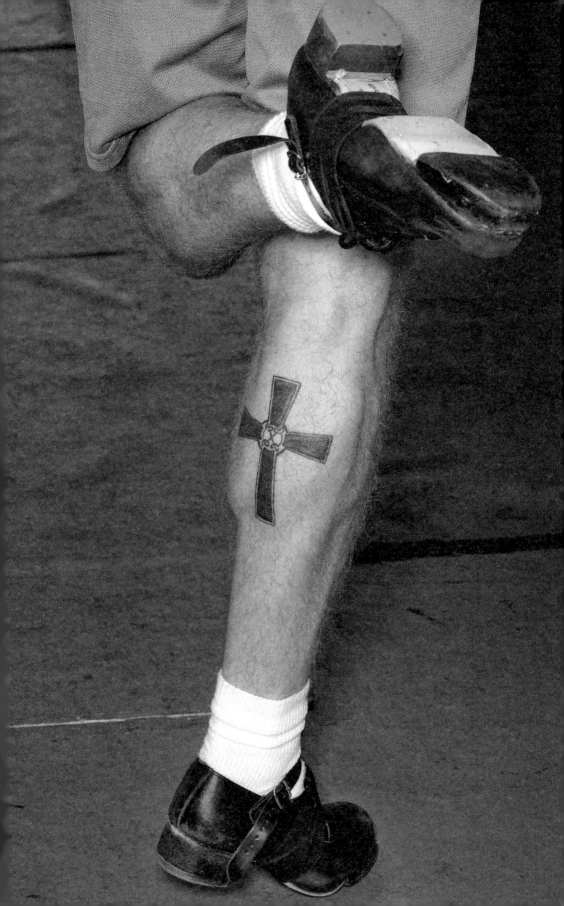

Some Numbers

COMINGS AND GOINGS

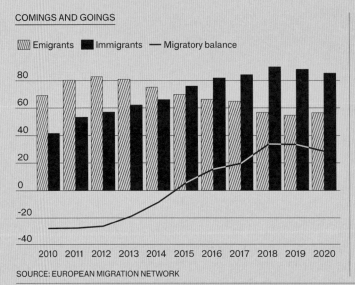

Legend: Emigrants | Immigrants | — Migratory balance

SOURCE: EUROPEAN MIGRATION NETWORK

PRODUCTIVE

GDP per hour worked, in US$, 2020

Ireland	**111.8**
Luxembourg	96.7
Norway	85.5
Denmark	75.4
USA	74.3
Switzerland	70.7
Austria	70.2
France	67.6
Netherlands	67.0
Germany	66.9
Italy	54.7

SOURCE: OECD

INTEGRATION

Share of respondents who believe immigrants are well integrated into their country (%), 2021

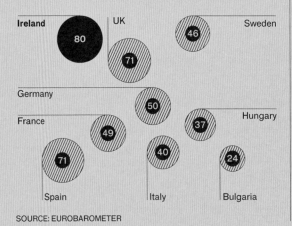

Ireland 80 | UK 71 | Sweden 46
Germany 50 | France 49 | Hungary 37
Spain 71 | Italy 40 | Bulgaria 24

SOURCE: EUROBAROMETER

OVERTAKING

GDP per capita in international $ (hypothetical currency based on purchasing power parity)

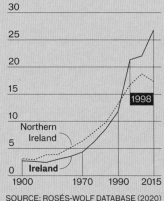

Northern Ireland
Ireland
1998

SOURCE: ROSÉS-WOLF DATABASE (2020)

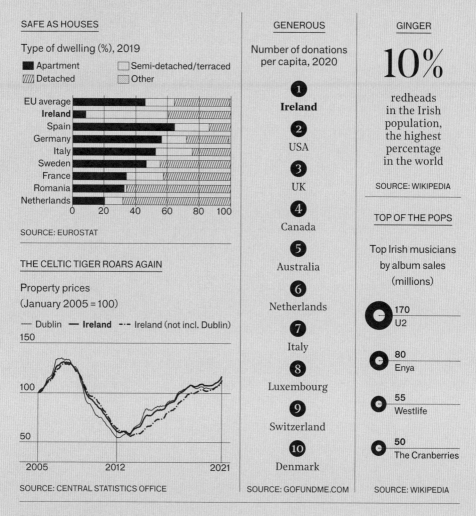

SAFE AS HOUSES

Type of dwelling (%), 2019

- ■ Apartment
- ▨ Detached
- ☐ Semi-detached/terraced
- ▤ Other

EU average	
Ireland	
Spain	
Germany	
Italy	
Sweden	
France	
Romania	
Netherlands	

0 20 40 60 80 100

SOURCE: EUROSTAT

THE CELTIC TIGER ROARS AGAIN

Property prices
(January 2005 = 100)

— Dublin — **Ireland** -·- Ireland (not incl. Dublin)

150

100

50

2005   2012   2021

SOURCE: CENTRAL STATISTICS OFFICE

GENEROUS

Number of donations
per capita, 2020

1 Ireland

2 USA

3 UK

4 Canada

5 Australia

6 Netherlands

7 Italy

8 Luxembourg

9 Switzerland

10 Denmark

SOURCE: GOFUNDME.COM

GINGER

10%

redheads
in the Irish
population,
the highest
percentage
in the world

SOURCE: WIKIPEDIA

TOP OF THE POPS

Top Irish musicians
by album sales
(millions)

170
U2

80
Enya

55
Westlife

50
The Cranberries

SOURCE: WIKIPEDIA

ENTH-EU-SIASTS

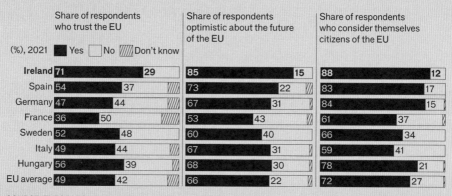

Share of respondents
who trust the EU

(%), 2021 ■ Yes ☐ No ▨ Don't know

	Yes	No	
Ireland	71	29	
Spain	54	37	
Germany	47	44	
France	36	50	
Sweden	52	48	
Italy	49	44	
Hungary	56	39	
EU average	49	42	

Share of respondents
optimistic about the future
of the EU

Yes	No	
85	15	
73	22	
67	31	
53	43	
60	40	
67	31	
68	30	
66	22	

Share of respondents
who consider themselves
citizens of the EU

Yes	No	
88	12	
83	17	
84	15	
61	37	
66	34	
59	41	
78	21	
72	27	

SOURCE: EUROBAROMETER

The authors Catherine Dunne (left)
and Caelainn Hogan at Catherine's Dublin home.

The Mass
Is Ended

CATHERINE DUNNE AND CAELAINN HOGAN

Over the course of just a few decades Ireland's once insular and conservative society has undergone a radical transformation. Two writers from different generations meet up in a Dublin garden to discuss the decline of the Catholic Church's influence, the dismantling of a system designed to oppress women and how Irish people have long shown themselves to be more progressive than their politicians.

9

There is an image from the recent Repeal the Eighth Amendment campaign that still moves me. Dozens of young women stand together on one of the bridges over Dublin's River Liffey. Their long banner with the word 'REPEAL' in huge letters flutters in the breeze. All of them are dressed in the flowing red robes and white bonnets made famous by the TV series of Margaret Atwood's *The Handmaid's Tale*.

It is a sunny day, everyone is in high good humour, the dramatic red and white of the young women's costumes is startling against the unusual blue of the sky.

I am in my mid-sixties when I gaze on this *tableau vivant*; my companion in these essays, Caelainn Hogan, is in her early thirties. She, too, tells me how struck she has been by the joyful and inclusive nature of this whole campaign.

But we are both conscious that we grew up in very different Irelands. We know how the legacy of that earlier country still lives on.

In May 2018, after thirty-eight years, the effective ban on abortion in this country – the Eighth Amendment to the Constitution – is removed. Throughout the campaign, women, often with their partners, tell stories of grief and pain, of sorrow and loss. Stories of hard choices. Stories of fighting for reproductive rights. The wall of silence that once engulfed this country begins, at last, to crack. At first a trickle then a deluge, the complex stories of women's lives begin to flood into the light.

Irish people – most of them, on this occasion – vote for compassion and understanding rather than the strictures of Catholic dogma. There are tears of joy and relief as women absorb the fact that at last, almost four decades later, the younger generations can now exercise their reproductive choices at home.

It hasn't always been like this.

*

Back in 1983 there had been a very different campaign. The Abortion Referendum of that year was toxic, divisive and bitter. 'The past is a foreign country,' the novelist L.P. Hartley once wrote, 'they do things differently there.' That is certainly true of Ireland. This country was, up until the 1990s, a deeply conservative Catholic state. Lawmakers bowed to bishops and archbishops. In every aspect of a citizen's life – education, health (particularly women's health), sexuality, marriage and children – the Church held sway.

In 1985, in what was perhaps one of the first acts of defiance of the Catholic authorities, the Irish government had approved the sale of contraceptives. A long battle had been waged to get to that point. In the mid-1970s I used to attend one of the family planning clinics in

CATHERINE DUNNE is the author of eleven published novels and one work of non-fiction, *An Unconsidered People* (2003; revised edition 2021), exploring the lives of Irish immigrants in 1950s London. Her novels include *The Things We Know Now*, recipient of the Giovanni Boccaccio International Prize for Fiction in 2013 and shortlisted for the Novel of the Year at the Irish Book Awards, *The Years That Followed*, longlisted for the International Dublin Literary Award in 2018 and *Come cade la luce* ('The Way the Light Falls'), shortlisted for the European Strega Prize for Fiction in 2019. Catherine received the Irish PEN Award for outstanding contribution to Irish literature in 2018 and in January 2021 was decorated as Cavaliere of the Order Stella d'Italia.

There is an old video cassette gathering dust somewhere that has me captured on its stretch of shiny film, brown and slick like river water, the reels that we used to untangle and wind back up as children. I am walking through a church in an off-white Holy Communion dress on my way back from the altar, my hands probably still in prayer, but all the while conspicuously and furiously chewing the host.

It wasn't that I was a child with an anti-clerical streak. The song about being raised up on eagle's wings was playing, and I wanted to sing along with it, so chewing the wafer seemed practical. Surely God wouldn't mind whether it dissolved or was masticated; the body of Christ ended up in the same belly. I remember the surprise when relatives laughed and pointed it out when they watched it back.

A generation before, though, it would have been seen as a real sin to chew the host. You had to let it melt respectfully away even if it stuck like gum to the roof of your mouth and you had to tease it down quietly with your tongue before swallowing.

I recently described this video to the author Catherine Dunne, sitting in her bright home in Dublin city filled with bookcases and artworks. We were meeting to speak about the difference between our generations when it came to religion in Ireland, but the housing crisis was the first thing we talked about, with me in my early thirties renting with three other people the same age or older, and with most people I know generally priced out of the life our parents had. My generation faced an ever-deepening economic inequality while growing up in an Ireland that was at least breaking free from a de facto theocracy, further pursuing opportunities and rights that were long fought for.

When she was in school Catherine had to learn to recite the catechism for her first communion, and to be caught chewing the wafer so you could sing would have been a source of shame and maybe punishment. 'That I could get a laugh about that as a child, you know, is quite phenomenal,' I said to her about chewing the body of Christ. 'To see that change over such a short period of time.'

*

I was born in Ireland's National Maternity Hospital in 1988, only a year after the country finally abolished the legal status of illegitimacy that stripped equal rights from children who were born to so-called 'unmarried mothers'. Condoms weren't fully legal here until the 1990s and divorce was only voted in when I was a few years into school. The Catholic Church had railed against these changes and tried to exert its once unparalleled authority over

CAELAINN HOGAN is an Irish journalist and writer. She has written for international newspapers and magazines covering issues of conflict, migration and marginalisation, reporting from Nigeria, South Africa and Syria during the civil war. Her articles have been published in *The New York Times Magazine*, *Harper's*, *The New Yorker*, *Vice*, the *Guardian*, Al Jazeera English, the *Irish Times* and the *Dublin Review*. In 2019 she published *Republic of Shame: How Ireland Punished 'Fallen Women' and Their Children* (Penguin) about the system of institutions run by the Catholic Church with the cooperation of the Irish state in which until very recent times 'unmarried mothers' were imprisoned and routinely abused and exploited. She is a recipient of the Arts Council of Ireland's 2021 Next Generation Artists Award.

Dublin. In order to circumvent the law the clinics at that time would accept a 'donation' from their patients in lieu of payment for contraceptives – along with the gratitude of thousands of young women who didn't want to get pregnant.

The 1985 law was a controversial one, indicating the strength of the relationship between Church and state. The close ties between the two would only begin to loosen when the revelation of systemic sexual abuse within the institution of the Church came to light. This entire country was convulsed by the evidence that emerged and kept emerging from the late 1980s on of the unchecked abuses perpetrated by paedophile priests against young boys and girls. The complicity of the Catholic institution in protecting its own abusers was laid bare: a criminal complicity that began with local priests and bishops and went all the way to the Vatican.

I completed a part-time course in journalism in the early 1990s established by a very well-known and well-connected priest, Fr Sean Fortune. I can still remember the sense of shock and revulsion all of us former students felt when the news eventually broke about his abuse of children. The Church authorities had failed, for years, to prevent this man having access to children, despite numerous anguished reports of his criminal behaviour.

He committed suicide in 1999 while awaiting trial.

There were other reasons, too, that the influence of Catholicism had begun to wane during the 1990s. Universal access to education was one. Sustained economic development was another. Membership of the EU meant an increasing awareness of lives lived in other countries. People had begun to travel more. Irish migrants brought new perspectives and different life experiences along with them as they returned home in increasing numbers. Global communication networks meant that discussions regarding equality and diversity in all its forms were accessed in this country, too.

Back in the early years of the 1980s, though, the influence of the Catholic Church was still pervasive enough to succeed in the campaign to insert a new article into the Irish Constitution. To this end it had had significant support from right-wing Christian organisations in the United States. The wording of this new Article 40.3.3 guaranteed that at all stages of pregnancy 'the right to life of the unborn' was 'equal to the right to life of the mother'.

The debates that followed were deeply troubling. Even in those days everyone was aware that women in this country had abortions. We all knew somebody who knew somebody who knew somebody else who had travelled to England on a 'shopping trip'. Or else, we were that 'somebody else' ourselves. But those stories were often whispered ones, shared over coffee or confided late at night to a sympathetic ear. In too many instances what felt like a shameful secret lay hidden, remaining unspoken for a lifetime.

The toxic divisions of the early 1980s, the hostility towards women who spoke up, spoke out, made me feel that Ireland was not a good place to be a woman. I wanted to leave. I set my sights on Canada: its equality legislation was light years ahead of Ireland's. I had worked there for a summer in my mid-twenties and loved its tolerance, its multicultural cities, its openness and its absence of Irish small-townness. I'd started to write when I was there in the late 1970s. I can still remember the cool, dim interior of what it considered the 'institution' of the family, even as the cover-up of clerical child sexual abuse and the cruelty of the religious-run institutions was being exposed.

Over the past decade investigation after investigation has been launched into this interconnected system of institutions, from the industrial schools to the Magdalene Laundries and most recently the mother-and-baby homes where pregnant women were sent, often made to work unpaid for months or years, and most were separated from their children (see 'Institutionalised Cruelty' on page 27). This system of

institutions 'disappeared' women and children who didn't fit the Church's ideal of a family and effectively sought to maintain the religious hierarchy's authority on sex outside of marriage.

I started writing my book *Republic of Shame* about these institutions in 2017 when a test excavation at the site of a former mother-and-baby home in Tuam, where more than eight hundred children died, showed that infants and children were buried in sewage chambers in the grounds, dating back to a time when the Bon Secours nuns ran it and the local council funded it. If not for the tireless work of a local historian, Catherine Corless, and the courage of families and survivors speaking out, the truth might never have been known. The state was forced to launch an investigation not just into Tuam but into the wider system

A children's blessing during the annual Harvest Mass at St Brigid's Church, Corofin, County Clare.

A statue of the Virgin Mary in Bracknagh, County Offaly.

my favourite library in Toronto. Perhaps it was writing that was drawing me back there, too.

But the visa application was turned down. I was bitterly disappointed. A few years later, in the way that these things sometimes happen, I was relieved. My mother became ill, and I knew then that Ireland was where I needed to be.

Nonetheless, it took some time for me to love the country again.

*

Accompanying the child-abuse scandals of the 1990s was the suffering of generations of Irish citizens who had followed their Church faithfully all their lives. Now everything needed to be questioned. The received wisdom of the past did not stand up to scrutiny. The idols were found to have feet of clay. One after another, certainties came crashing down. It emerged, for example, that the Irish priest and bishop who had stood at the altar beside Pope John Paul II during his 1979 visit to Ireland, both of them exhorting the huge congregation to be better Irish Catholics, had each fathered secret children of his own.

The pain of the faithful was real, raw, palpable, particularly for those who belonged to older generations. My Catholic faith, such as it was, had dissolved years earlier. It did not survive a year – 1972–3, my first time away from home – living and teaching in Franco's Spain. It had been a childlike faith to begin with; the sort of inherited, untested, blinkered belief of the innocent, a faith that, once challenged, either becomes stronger or fades away.

of mother-and-baby home institutions across the country. The deeply flawed final report, published in 2021 during a pandemic lockdown, with survivors not even being given a hard copy to read before a rushed state apology, found that more than nine thousand children died in these institutions and more than a hundred thousand women and children were kept behind the walls of these so-called 'homes'.

For people my age it was the latest horror in a litany of brutal truths emerging about how Church and state treated people whom legislation and doctrine made vulnerable and marginalised; this was the Ireland of the very recent past, and these institutions were still operating during our lifetimes.

*

The same year I began the book the country was looking ahead to a referendum on legalising abortion, with countless people speaking out about their own experiences of being forced to travel to access healthcare and stigmatised for their choice (see 'Citizens' Assemblies: Experiments in Democracy' on page 139), and I would speak that year to my mum for the first time about her own abortions. I began speaking to survivors of the religious-run institutions who were told by the nuns there that their labour pains were payment for their sin and about being separated from their children.

A few years earlier the Marriage Equality Referendum in Ireland had also passed by a landslide. One thing that I particularly remembered about the campaign was the debate that happened around who gets to be a family. People within the Church, people campaigning against marriage equality, had brought up the question of children, thinking that it

would be a strong argument, but it backfired. Irish people were finally saying, 'No, you don't get to tell us who's a family any more.' It brought to the surface a lot of stories about how, often through actions by the religious-run institutions, families in Ireland had been torn apart and how others had been denied the right to the protections of a family under the law.

I was in Geneva at the World Health Assembly when the vote for marriage equality took place. I remember people working for the UN saying how great it was and that, of course, it'll pass. But everyone I knew, even people who had been canvassing non-stop, still had this fear that a silent conservative majority that didn't share our hopes and experiences of a changing Ireland would vote it down. When the vote for 'Yes' passed by such a margin it was like suddenly we could trust each other. So many women and girls were sent away to the mother-and-baby institutions by priests, doctors, social workers, crisis pregnancy agencies, by their own families, by parents who were told by nuns and priests that it was best for them or who feared what the neighbours would think. The moral judgement the Church enshrined in people made them fear each other. I remember a friend of mine, who had come out when we were all in school and who still faced hate for who he loved while growing up, weeping with relief and joy in a nightclub at the first Pride after the vote. He then went on to campaign in every way he could for abortion rights. I think of friends whose mothers raised them alone and who spoke about the solidarity of gay friends they lived with; homosexuality still criminalised until 1993 and women effectively criminalised in so many ways for having sex outside marriage.

A vote for marriage equality and then

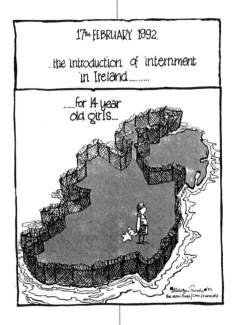

Mine disappeared, leaving behind only a small flame of fury, a presence that could still ignite and which burned all too brightly during the revelations of the 1990s. The collapse of the institutional reputation of the Church would continue to form the seed-bed, the ashes, from which a new and secular Irish phoenix was preparing to rise.

Part of this seed-bed was the X-Case of 1992.

In February of that year a fourteen-year-old child, pregnant as a result of rape, had travelled to Britain with her parents for an abortion. She was distressed to the point of being suicidal. Her parents had reported the rape to the Irish police (the Garda) and wished to bring foetal matter back home as evidence to help convict the rapist – a respectable, middle-aged family acquaintance. The attorney general was informed of the parents' plan and imme-diately obtained an interim injunction stopping the teenager from terminating her pregnancy. Once they were informed of the injunction the parents obediently returned to Ireland with their bewildered, terrified pregnant daughter.

A prominent cartoon of the time shows a child with a teddy bear standing on a map of Ireland facing the Irish Sea. All her escape routes are blocked by barbed wire.

The X-Case caused public outrage. It seemed that the impact of our black-and-white abortion law had finally seeped into the public consciousness at large, and young and old – on both sides of the divide, it has to be said – took to the streets to make their voices heard.

The law stood.

Nonetheless, the strength of public feeling was enough to widen the crack that had already occurred in the bastion of traditional Catholicism. Conversations began to get louder in kitchens and pubs and cafés and workplaces all over the country. More stories began to be told, more secrets were shared.

Perhaps things weren't so black and white after all; these stories suggested

for legal abortion led to the breaking of more silences. When the pope last visited Ireland it was shortly after the vote to legalise abortion, and I walked through Dublin with two women, two pilgrims, heading to the mass in the Phoenix Park. The last time a pope visited he was greeted onstage at one mass by a priest and a bishop who both had secret children. Those two women walking to the papal mass told me proudly, with smiles on their faces, that they had voted 'Yes' to repeal Ireland's ban on abortion. The women also remembered growing up near a religious-run institution down the road from my own family home, where hundreds of children were held for adoption, most of them branded 'illegitimate' children by the law and born in mother-and-baby homes, many of those adoptions illegal and likely forced. These women wanted the culture of secrecy around those institutions to end and for adopted people, who were searching for their roots, their original identities and were still being denied access to their birth certificates and records by the Irish state, to get justice. Noelle Brown, an adoption-rights activist I spoke to who was born in the Bessborough mother-and-baby institution, spent years looking into her own background. She campaigned for both marriage equality and abortion rights but also sees the right of adopted people to their identity and the end of that culture of secrecy in Ireland as an issue of equality.

*

My generation grew up watching the walls of the theocracy crumble, but people my own age and younger were also born in religious-run institutions to which 'unmarried mothers' were sent and separated from their children, sometimes institutionalised and exploited by religious orders for life. At apartment viewings, at house parties, over dinners and pints, hungover with friends in the sun, I had endless spontaneous conversations with people I knew and people I had just met about the women they knew who had been disappeared or still carried the secret of what had been done to them, the baby they never saw again, the information they were searching for. While writing *Republic of Shame* I met people my own age born in these institutions who were only beginning to search for answers and still being denied the right to their identity and information along with the daughters and sons of survivors who were continuing their parents' search for justice. Jess Kavanagh, an Irish singer, spoke about finding a 'linguistic arsenal' to try to articulate how the status of illegitimacy impacted her own family and her own life, her mother adopted through an institution and a dash on her own birth certificate where her father's name should have been, left blank because of the shame enforced through doctrine and legislation. Another woman born only a few years before me, separated from her mother as a baby in a religious-run institution, had to spend hours in a register office searching through thousands of names in ledgers trying to find her mother, because the Irish state still denies her the right to her identity and origins. My generation has seen the unquestionable authority of the Church in Ireland challenged but recognises the ongoing harm that it caused this country and the impact it had on our own families. People of our parents' generation speak of beatings and deliberate humiliation by nuns and priests in schools and having to bow or step off the street to let members of the religious orders pass.

that maybe we spend most of our lives navigating shades of grey.

*

Fast-forward exactly twenty years to the death of Savita Halappanavar in 2012. Ms Halappanavar, a young Indian woman – a dentist living and working in this country – was admitted to a hospital in the west of Ireland in the throes of a miscarriage. She was told that the foetus would not survive. She was devastated: this was a much-longed-for pregnancy. Deeply distressed, she accepted that she was losing the baby and requested a termination – not once but several times. All her requests were denied. A foetal heartbeat was still present, she was told. Such a termination would be against Irish law. She subsequently died of sepsis. She was thirty-one.

Ms Halappanavar's husband, Praveen, hoped afterwards that perhaps her experience might help to change the law in Ireland. I believe it did, but why did she have to die? I joined the thousands of people, men and women, who took to the streets that November, fuelled by a raging sense of injustice and anger and grief. Women felt, once again, like second-class citizens.

In May 2018 when the referendum passed by 66.4 per cent to 33.6 per cent – almost an exact reversal of the 1983 vote – and the way was paved for new legislation, Ms Halappanavar's father, Andanappa Yalagi, said, 'We are really, really happy. We have one last request, that the new law, that it is called "Savita's law". It should be named for her.'

Savita Halappanavar's story, along with that of the X-Case and so many others, moved people towards compassion and understanding. The stories that characterised this latest referendum of 2018 symbolised another significant opening up of Irish society, another breach in the wall of silence.

The tragic stories became, ultimately, more fuel to the fire of secularisation. A fire that eventually led to the new law of 2018, a law that permits abortion up to twelve weeks.

Anecdotal evidence, however, shows that, despite this new law, women are finding that in practice terminations are still difficult to access, particularly if they have just passed the twelve-week cut-off point. The law is also restrictive in its definition of 'fatal foetal abnormality', meaning that some women are still forced to travel outside Ireland to secure the termination they need.

*

Caelainn tells me that she remembers the Divorce Referendum of the mid-1990s – or rather, as a seven-year old child she remembers some of the images, some of the intensity of feeling around that time. She recalls the opposition posters, in particular: their lurid colours with taglines such as 'Hello Divorce ... Bye Bye Daddy ... Vote NO!'

I remember it, too. I remember campaigning, dropping leaflets through letter boxes, having long conversations on doorsteps. Those weeks had an enormous impact on me. I had also been active during the first campaign, and I was both struck and saddened, almost a decade later, that I was hearing the same trapped, anguished stories all over again. The cruelty of it all: that denial of a second chance. Eventually, in 1997 the experience of campaigning in both referenda became the inspiration for my first novel, *In the Beginning*.

An absolute prohibition on divorce, along with the ban on abortion, had also

But that older generation often tells us 'it was the times'. The younger generations now following us and carving out a new future on this island have no time for this excuse, and whenever I've been involved in talks with students and young people the anger at what the Church and state did to women and children is palpable. The first time many of them voted they achieved radical changes that rejected the religious conservativism in this country.

*

In 2016 the census in the Republic of Ireland found that Roman Catholics accounted for 78.3 per cent of the population compared with 84.2 per cent during the previous census in 2011. This has dropped from a peak of 94.9 per cent in 1961, during a decade when at one point close to 90 per cent of all children born 'out of wedlock' were taken from their mothers for adoption.

My generation is often told they can't fully understand what it meant to live in a country where the Church was seen as an unquestionable authority that could never be challenged. 'There was no sex education,' Catherine says, 'but I do remember some of the strictures that were laid down, and one of them certainly was that men were unable to control their urges and that, therefore, it was a woman's job, it was her duty, to make sure that she kept things under control. If anything did get out of control, in Ireland it was the woman's fault.'

When Catherine moved to what we call 'secondary school' at the age of around twelve, it was the first year of free education in Ireland. She remembers discussions at home between her dad, an electrician, and her stay-at-home mother about how this could change the futures of Irish children like her and the new

choices it created. The Irish Constitution still states that a woman's place is in the home. Éamon De Valera, an early leader of the Republic and architect of the constitution – whose own son would facilitate illegal adoptions of Irish children born to 'unmarried mothers' – famously spoke of his vision of an island populated by 'comely maidens', not the headstrong women who had fought for independence. Because of the marriage bar, once a woman was married she had to give up work. Both of Catherine's parents left school at fourteen and went out into the world of work. As well as being a writer, Catherine spent years as a secondary-school teacher and was keenly aware of the changes that started happening within the system, a sign of the theocracy breaking down. In the 1980s interdenominational schools slowly began to 'blossom', as she described it, a radical break from the domination of the Church over education. A colleague of hers was agitated by this, asking why secular schools were needed when the population was majority Catholic, although schools run by the Catholic Church could technically refuse students if they weren't baptised. 'That was another part of the opening-up,' she said. 'I've always thought that there are two elements that keep a country, any country, under the grip of any kind of fundamentalism. When you no longer control education and when you can't control influences from abroad, these two things together begin to spell the end of whatever dynasty has been created.'

I remember jokes in school about going on a 'shopping trip' to England, a euphemism for girls having to travel away to access legal abortion. I studied mostly in Catholic-ethos schools and remember little in the way of sex education, but I

been enshrined in our 1937 constitution. A campaign to remove that ban in 1986 had failed. The second attempt in 1996 was successful – just. It was passed by a margin of 50.28 per cent to 49.72 per cent.

Once again, during that divorce campaign couples had come forward to tell their stories. At the time 75,000 marriages, according to official statistics, had irretrievably broken down. No doubt there were others, unofficially, sharing that same leaky boat. The insulting implication of the opposition posters on lamp posts all over the country was that fathers would desert their families wholesale if Ireland legalised divorce. The Catholic Church was fierce in its opposition to the proposed legislation, claiming that marriages should remain intact even if the relationship had broken down for good. To stay together would be a good example to society, the bishops claimed. And to refrain from remarriage, they stressed, would be 'a particularly heroic sign by those who, even when abandoned by their partner, with the strength and faith of Christian hope have not entered a new union, these spouses too give an authentic witness of fidelity, of which the world today has great need'.

Once again, as in 1985, the state authorities clashed publicly with the Church. This time, however, the tone was noticeably more critical. The Office of the Taoiseach (prime minister) of the day, John Bruton, noted that broken marriage was 'a growing reality in Ireland today which the Catholic Church, despite its extensive influence on the opinions of many, has not so far been able to reverse'. The government statement accused the bishops' attitude of being 'uncompromising and ungenerous' and that it 'suggests that the hierarchy has greater faith in the value of social engineering than in the responsibility of the individual conscience'.

It was a watershed moment. The government, publicly and unequivocally, told the Catholic authorities that Irish adults had the right to make up their own minds.

In 1996 it felt as though Ireland was finally beginning to grow up.

*

We would revisit this kind of Catholic rhetoric, however, in the run-up to the Thirty-Fourth Amendment to the Constitution (Marriage Equality) Act 2015. We've already seen the sea change in Irish social attitudes that began in the late 1980s. Silences began to fracture. Marriage breakdown was becoming more visible, less shameful. Homosexuality was decriminalised in 1993. Divorce became a reality in 1996 – and no, the entire society did not collapse.

Ireland still has one of the lowest divorce rates in the EU. Eurostat figures for 2015 show that 0.7 divorces per 1,000 of the population took place in this country, as against 1.4 per 1,000 in Italy, for example, over the same period.

The attitude of the official Catholic Church towards same-sex marriage is unequivocal – despite Pope Francis's question in 2013, 'Who am I to judge gay people?' As late as March 2021 the Congregation for the Doctrine of the Faith (CDF) said, with reference to gay marriage, that it was 'impossible' for God to 'bless sin'. However, the CDF did note the 'positive elements' in same-sex relationships.

The passing of the Marriage Equality Act 2015 in Ireland came before the Abortion Referendum in 2018, but they were both results of the same process of

A crowd gathers in front of the Dáil Éireann, the lower house of the Irish parliament, to demonstrate following the death in childbirth of Savita Halappanavar.

never felt a pressure to be religious or that I wasn't able to question what was being taught.

My generation faced an exodus from Ireland during the last global recession, but the conservatism and repression that forced countless people to leave the island in earlier decades was finally waning. While writing *Republic of Shame* I spoke to women who had left Ireland for the UK after finding out they were pregnant not only to access legal abortion across the water but also because many were hoping to be able to keep their child and raise them away from prying eyes. This was so common that social workers in England had a shorthand term for it: PFI (Pregnant from Ireland). Many pregnant women were sent back by Catholic 'rescue' societies to the mother-and-baby institutions in Ireland, separated from their children while in these so-called 'homes' before being sent back again to England on a boat or a plane. Many young women born in a home and institutionalised for their entire youth, in industrial or reformatory schools or Magdalene Laundries, left for the UK as soon as they had a chance to get away or were released once the state stopped paying for them at sixteen, believing it was the only way to escape from the stigma and further institutionalisation.

*

'In other countries, such as Italy or Spain or France, where Catholicism would the liberalisation of Irish social attitudes. It was a reflection of a society that had become much more diverse since the 1990s.

For example, during that economically heady ten-year period from 1997 to 2007 a significant transformation in the make-up of our population was taking place. Ireland has always been a country whose citizens have emigrated in waves – our worldwide diaspora is evidence of that. If we look at the emotive definition of diaspora – those who claim even distant Irish ancestry and who like to identify as Irish – then the number is somewhere around seventy million. From Famine times to recession times, Ireland has exported its people.

But membership of the EU meant that there was a significant increase in immigration flows in that same decade 1997–2007. Our Central Statistics Office tells me, for example, 'there was a total of 420,000 non-Irish nationals living in Ireland in April 2006, representing 188 different countries. While the vast majority of these people were from a very small number of countries – 82 per cent from just ten – there was also a remarkable diversity in the range of countries represented.' In 1998 that figure for non-Irish nationals living in Ireland was lower than fifty thousand. Eight years later it was eight times that amount. The numbers vary from study to study, but according to official government documents there was an 'average non-Irish population of 14.9 per cent for all Irish towns over 1,500 inhabitants in 2016'. That was the average: there were, of course, several very surprised villages in rural Ireland that suddenly saw their population increase radically, and there were also those towns that remained relatively untouched. Immigrants, as always, will follow the work.

And I would argue that that growing diversity in our population was yet another of the contributing factors to the waves of social change in this country since the 1990s.

The years preceding and those immediately following the passing of the Marriage Equality Act 2015 brought into the light some very interesting – and painful – questions about what it means to be a family. The Church continued to advocate that it takes a man and a woman to raise a child. At the same time ongoing research was, once again, excavating the history of Church-run institutions that had brutalised young pregnant women for generations, that had trafficked the children born to them. A Church that was responsible for so many illegal adoptions with the complicity of the state. It was hard to see where their moral authority to define 'the sacred nature of the family' came from.

Caelainn Hogan has done invaluable research on this iniquitous system of Church–state complicity. Her 2019 book *Republic of Shame* illuminates the philosophy that underpinned the shunning of 'sinful' women and the resultant breaking apart of so many families.

*

Ireland has come a long way in the last thirty years. But many battles still remain. Many important conversations are still to be had; many more stories need to be brought out into the light.

So where to now?

As a child of the 1950s I looked around me in astonishment at the sudden affluence of what was called our 'Celtic Tiger' economy, a boom that lasted for over a decade, starting in the mid-1990s and have been the dominant religion, that marriage between Church and state was not to the same extent as it was here,' Catherine noted. 'Italian journalists or readers, particularly women, used to look at me in appalled disbelief when I'd tell them that it took until 2018 for us even to have a very restrictive abortion law in place, and they don't get it. They just don't get it.' She describes the Ireland that she grew up in as inward looking and insular, a country that defined itself as being 'not English' while taking time to acknowledge itself as European. In reality, the system of religious-run institutions that were the foundations of the theocracy in Ireland were operated by religious orders that had mother houses in France and England. The system also had its origins in the workhouse system imposed by the colonial British Poor Laws before partition and independence, a system that institutionalised the vulnerable and separated families. A religious order based in England operated three major mother-and-baby institutions in Ireland where thousands of infants and children died, buried in unmarked graves. Catherine remembered the equality legislation that was pushed through within the EU and held Ireland to a new standard when it came to human rights. It was the international outrage over the deaths and unmarked burials at Tuam, after the journalist Alison O'Reilly broke the news, that made 'a lot of people here sit up', as Catherine described it. 'One of the ways in which the Church had always got away with everything was not only the insistence on secrecy but also this kind of national sense of superiority that we were always so much better, so much more moral than people across the water.'

In the summer of 2021 Catholic churches on Indigenous land in Canada went up in flames, burned to the ground after findings that hundreds of Indigenous children were buried in unmarked graves on the grounds of religious-run 'training' schools that separated them from their communities and sought to assimilate them forcibly into a repressive ideal of society and to become what the state considered useful or acceptable. Many people in Ireland wondered why the same had never happened here, despite the exposed horror of clerical child abuse, the cover-up by the Church of that abuse for so many decades, the incarceration of women and children in prison-like institutions, the separation of children from their mothers. The Commission to Inquire into Child Abuse in Ireland, which issued its report more than a decade ago now, motivated other countries to launch similar investigations, and it feels like there is still an international reckoning with this legacy needed – *The Handmaid's Tale* is, after all, based on real injustices against women around the world, and Margaret Atwood herself held up a copy of my book during an event in Dublin, lending her words for the cover of the paperback published in 2020, comparing Ireland's institutions with Gilead and concluding, 'At least in *The Handmaid's Tale* they value babies, mostly. Not so in the true stories here.'

'Ireland was seen as this sort of bastion of Catholic values. We were seen as a Catholic country,' Catherine said during our conversation, 'so for Irish people to be breaking silence about abuse within the Church was, I think, significant.'

The deference that remains towards the Catholic Church in Ireland is rooted in a belief that the religious orders gave us our hospitals and schools through pure charity – and where would we be without *them*? But the Church built its empire ending abruptly in 2008. When the global crash happened Ireland suffered badly, along with Portugal, Italy, Greece and Spain, the so-called PIIGS of Europe. It was a huge step backwards in so many ways, a stark reminder that housing, health and education have to be a state's top priorities. The years of austerity that followed cut essential services to the bone.

There are many other inequalities to be addressed, too, not least the treatment of refugees and asylum seekers in our current profit-making system of Direct Provision (see 'Asylum Seekers in a Land of Emigration' on page 26), a system that the UNHCR has condemned as recently as October 2020. It has called for immediate, urgent reforms to be implemented in all aspects of this inhumane system.

There is still a gender pay gap. Our health service is straining at the seams, particularly since Covid-19. Mental health services, for young people in particular, are inadequate. Housing is the biggest single issue for young people today, with average rents per month for a modest apartment in the capital – where most of the jobs are – costing between €1,500 and €2,000 ($1,730–$2,300). Since the economic crash of 2008 not enough houses have been built in this country: scarcity of supply is driving house prices up even further, effectively locking out a whole generation of young people who will never be able to afford their own homes.

And the battle with the Catholic Church is not over yet. As I write, there is an ongoing controversy regarding Catholic ownership of the land on which the new state maternity hospital is to be built. This Church refusal to pass the land back to the state so that a world-class maternity hospital can be built is the latest move in the Church's struggle to maintain control over medical and budgetary decisions.

The stand-off between Church and state continues.

*

As we emerge – slowly, very slowly – from the pandemic, I make an act of will to be optimistic. I take heart from the fact that, increasingly over the decades, Irish people are ahead of their politicians in every important aspect of social inclusion. The Citizens' Assemblies in particular show how there is the instinct and the will to create a better society for all (see 'Citizens' Assemblies: Experiments in Democracy' on page 139). To be inclusive, and welcoming, and fair.

It will mean eternal vigilance. We must all be ready to fight for the rights of those whose voices often remain unheard, even – perhaps particularly – when the granting of those rights may not affect us directly.

But I take comfort from the fact that we have become much more willing as a nation to listen to difficult stories, to accept that we often navigate our lives not by black-and-white rules but moving through shades of grey. In addition, there are two images above all that stay with me and comfort me.

The first is of the dozens of young women in their *Handmaid's Tale* outfits as they occupy the bridge across the River Liffey. The second is of the elegant grounds of Dublin Castle on that day in May 2015 when the Marriage Equality Referendum result is announced and Ireland says 'Yes' to gay marriage, continuing to forge this country into a society in which we can all belong. I can still see the riot of colour produced by dozens of rainbow flags waving joyfully in the bright air of a summer's day in Dublin. ✒

'My mother remembers parents at my school worrying about whether a dictionary should be allowed in the classroom because in the end that is how we learned about sex, by looking up the word.'

in Ireland and its institutions through public money, through the collection basket at mass, through the donations big and small, through state funding, through state contracts that sent the laundry of civil servants to be washed by women incarcerated by the nuns. At the same time the Catholic hierarchy opposed free and nationalised public services such as healthcare for women and children. The religious orders that ran the Magdalene Laundries and mother-and-baby homes now operate the largest private health-care groups in the country and some of the largest in the world.

Since I was a child in Guardian Angels' National School, chewing the host so I could sing, Ireland has gone through radical change, but the economic inequality that leaves single mothers forced into institutional emergency home-less accommodation and still stigma-tised as a 'burden' on the taxpayer, the congregated settings that people with disabilities are still forced to live in, the discrimination against people of colour and people from the Irish Traveller community, who were treated even more harshly within religious-run institutions and denied their heritage, are part of the ongoing legacy of what I called the 'shame-industrial complex'.

My mother remembers parents at my school worrying about whether a dictionary should be allowed in the class-room because in the end that is how we learned about sex, by looking up the word.

The vast majority of Ireland's schools are still under the influence of the Catholic Church, and young people I speak to have still grown up with little or no sex educa-tion. Until recently there was a baptism barrier in place for many schools. Catherine sent her son to a non-denom-inational Educate Together school, and I attended one of those myself for a few years, meeting friends who expanded my understanding of the world and whose families were outside of the Church's ideal. For the next generations we owe them access to services that are truly public and free from a doctrine of shame and silence. 🐦

FRANCIS WHO?

Estimated size of congregations at papal masses in the Phoenix Park, Dublin

🙏 = 10,000 faithful

1979
Pope John Paul II
1,250,000

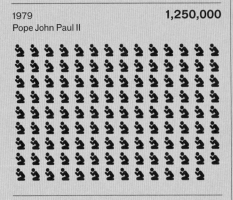

2018
Pope Francis
130,000

SOURCE: STATISTA

Religious affiliation in the RoI by age (%), 2017

- ■ Roman Catholic
- ▨ No religion
- ☐ Other religion

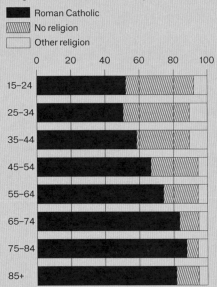

SOURCE: BBC

ASYLUM SEEKERS IN A LAND OF EMIGRATION

'Would the last one to leave please turn out the lights?' they used to joke in a wry take on the depopulation of Ireland, which had been a land of emigration since the first and most famous exodus during the Great Famine of the mid-19th century. It was only in the 21st century that the trend reversed, and in 2021 the population of the island of Ireland returned to 1851 levels, although still below the figure for 1841, when the population was at its highest. Net migration (including Irish citizens returning home) has been positive since 2015, and the number of foreign-born residents is on a constant upwards trajectory, with significant communities hailing from Poland, the UK (especially post-Brexit) and the Baltic States but also groups from outside Europe such as Nigerians and Brazilians. According to Eurobarometer, immigrants are better integrated in Ireland than anywhere else in Europe, a claim indirectly confirmed by the absence of anti-immigration parties in Parliament, in spite of the rapid relative increase in the numbers of foreign residents (13 per cent in 2021, of whom a minority are non-white). The sore point is the Direct Provision system for asylum-seeker accommodation, which was established in 1999 as a 'temporary measure'. People in the system are housed in centres run for profit by private companies under rules that keep them entirely dependent on the system. They receive €38.80 ($45) a week but are not allowed to work, go to school or do anything else apart from wait for their application to be processed. In theory the maximum wait is six months, but in reality the average is two years – and can be up to twelve in some cases. The system has been criticised by human rights charities and the UN as arbitrary and unnecessarily cruel. In February 2021 the government announced a plan for a complete reform of the system by 2024.

In Ireland the system of (re)educational institutions for women and children who did not conform to the idea of the Catholic family, funded by public money and run by religious organisations, displayed different degrees of cruelty depending on the group of people in their 'care'. Orphaned and abandoned children were shut away in **industrial schools**, where, according to a 2009 investigative commission report, they were subjected to physical, psychological and sexual abuse as well as other barbarities such as clinical trials for vaccines and experimental medicines, all under the supervision of the Department of Education. Unmarried women expecting babies, meanwhile, were sent away to give birth in **mother-and-baby homes**, where they had to stay for a year and carry out unpaid work in return for services rendered. At the end of the year the mothers left, but their children remained with the nuns until they were sent for adoption or into foster care (often without any consent sought) – or to the aforementioned industrial schools. In 2017 a mass grave was discovered in the grounds of one of these homes in the town of Tuam, County Galway, containing the remains of around eight hundred children. After analysing civil registry data, local historian Catherine Corless had noticed there were children missing and had an idea where to dig. Finally, there were the **Magdalene Laundries**, established to 'reform' fallen women, like the biblical figure Mary Magdalene from whom they took their inspiration. Initially the sinners (many of them teenagers) were often prostitutes, but over time any number of ways to 'fall' were devised: 'recidivist' unwed mothers and victims of rape or, more generally, girls who refused to conform to the prevailing morality. The institutions were genuine industrial laundries run for profit on the back of forced labour and with government contracts. The living and working conditions were extremely harsh, and abuse – including sexual abuse – was commonplace. There are no accurate figures for how many women found themselves in these institutions over their 150-year history, but estimates are in the region of thirty thousand. The last Magdalene Laundry closed in 1996 following the discovery in 1993 – by chance this time – of another mass grave when the nuns at a laundry in Dublin sold part of their grounds to a property developer in order to recoup the money from a loss-making investment.

Peat piled high near the Edenberry Power Station, County Offaly.

BOGLAND

WILLIAM ATKINS

Before becoming a driver of economic development in the Irish Midlands, peat bogs were an undesirable feature of the landscape, considered almost a national embarrassment. Then peat extraction became a source of jobs and fuel, but at the cost of severe damage to the ecology of the region. So the industry is now being dismantled, and the hope is that the bogs, with their remarkable ability to store carbon, will become another weapon in the arsenal of ways to help keep in check the warming of the climate.

29

The sky above Lodge Bog was a tarnished silver, and four crows tumbled across it like blown cinders. It was a scoured, shelterless place, a realm of few verticals and uncertain horizons, the kind of environment humankind has tended to avoid. And yet the bog was flourishing, abounding with life. To stand there felt like standing on the back of some vast recumbent mammal.

Lodge Bog is part of the Bog of Allen, a 960-square-kilometre swathe of ancient peatland in the Irish Midlands. A thousand years ago Lodge Bog was a lake. Over the centuries that lake became shallower as it accumulated silt from incoming watercourses. Vegetation encroached from its banks, replacing open water with reeds and lilies. As these plants died and sank the water grew shallower still, swampier, until a person could, with care, wade across it. A few hundred years more and the swamp had transformed into a fen, solider under foot, dominated by rushes, grasses and mosses. Year by year these plants also died, forming peat – a wet, fibrous, brown-black mass – until the surface of the fen rose in a dome above the level of the surrounding land. A raised bog had formed. Today there might be ten metres of peat between a raised bog's living surface and the clay, gravel or limestone underneath. The oldest, blackest, bottom-most peat might have been laid down eight millennia before the birth of Christ.

I was joined at Lodge Bog by Tristram Whyte, a freshwater ecologist with an outdoorsman's complexion and the cautious manner of someone accustomed to stalking flighty animals. Whyte works for the Irish Peatland Conservation Council (IPCC), a four-person organisation established in 1982 to protect a representative sample of the country's peatlands. Its offices are located in converted stables on nearby Lullymore Island, a rare zone of solid, fertile, mineral land amid the surrounding bogs. For centuries the 'island' was a place of refuge, connected to the outside world by a handful of hidden causeways. Its earliest settlement was a monastery founded in the 5th century and purportedly visited by St Patrick, whose 'footprint' – a heel-shaped dent – is still visible on a limestone boulder.

It was early autumn, and the bog, like the trees we could see on Lullymore, was relinquishing its green. Its colours were now khaki, beige, gold, crimson, ginger and – where peat was exposed or water had pooled – molasses brown or oily black. Small hummocks supported species that favour drier ground: russet-stemmed bog cotton, whose fluffy white bolls would constellate the landscape in spring; grey-green heather, or ling, which in August would crown the knolls with blooms of royal purple; devil's matchstick, with its livid pustules of scarlet fruit; and tiny, tentacled, carnivorous sundew, its glue-trap leaves primed to enfold insects. The wetter areas were dense with sphagnum moss, the bog's dominant and formative vegetation, its stems tangling

WILLIAM ATKINS is a British writer, editor and journalist. He writes for *Granta* magazine, the *Guardian*, *Harper's*, the *Financial Times* and *The New York Times*. His first book, *The Moor: A Journey into the English Wilderness* (Faber and Faber, 2014) was shortlisted for the Thwaites Wainwright Prize. He followed this up with *The Immeasurable World: Journeys in Desert Places* (Faber and Faber, 2018), which won the Stanford Dolman Travel Book of the Year award in 2019. His latest book, published by Faber and Faber in 2022, is *Exiles: Three Island Journeys*.

John Hogan (left) and Michael Nilan
collect peat near the village
of Ballyvaughan, County Clare.

deep into the water. So absorbent is sphagnum that during the First World War it was harvested by the ton for use as a surgical dressing.

I followed Whyte across a duckboard pathway the IPCC had installed towards the centre of the thirty-five-hectare bog. He crouched to examine the plant life. 'You've got your ling here, you've got sphagnum, this is *magellanicum* – you see how it's got a very stellate capitulum?' He pointed to the star-shaped head of a particular species of sphagnum. 'And that's *papillosum*, another species of sphagnum. We have bog cotton,

Eriophorum vaginatum, and see these little things like barley? That's bog asphodel; the Latin is *Narthecium ossifragum* ...'

Despite the profusion visible to Whyte's knowledgeable eye, the source of Lodge Bog's ecological value is its relative sparseness. 'Because everything's so specialised you get fewer species,' Whyte said. Many of those species, like the sundew, live nowhere else. This unique flora, I reminded myself, once covered almost the entire Bog of Allen.

Under normal conditions a plant removes carbon dioxide from the atmosphere through photosynthesis; when it drops its leaves or it dies, that carbon is returned to the atmosphere through decomposition. But things are different in a bog. In anaerobic, waterlogged conditions plants die without rotting. Rather than returning to the atmosphere the

The peat cutter Anthony Carrig
at the bog in Doonagore, Doolin,
County Clare.

carbon is stored. This means that bogs exert a net cooling effect on the climate. It also explains peat's historical use as a fuel source, both in domestic hearths and, more recently, on an industrial scale by Bord na Móna, the energy company whose excavated bogs have dominated the Midlands since the late 1940s. Today it is one of the region's principal employers.

Peatlands like those managed by the Bord, as the company is commonly known, are the largest carbon stores not only in Ireland but anywhere on the terrestrial planet. In all, they contain roughly twice the carbon of the world's forests. Estimates vary, but one report suggests there are 455 billion tonnes of carbon in the northern hemisphere's peatlands alone, equal to roughly half the carbon in the atmosphere. When a bog is drained or otherwise disturbed – in the course of commercial extraction, or domestic cutting, or agricultural improvement – the peat begins to dry and decompose, releasing the carbon it has accumulated over thousands of years. A two-metre-deep hectare of active peatland is estimated to extract almost a tonne of carbon from the air per year and to store up to eight thousand tonnes overall. If drained, that hectare would release an estimated six tonnes of carbon dioxide each year.

Since the founding of the Turf Development Board (the Bord's predecessor) in 1933, peat has become a crucial power source in Ireland; during the oil crisis of the early 1970s it provided as much as 40 per cent of the country's electricity. But peat has never been an efficient fuel – a recent assessment found that it accounted for less than 8 per cent of national electricity production but as much as 20 per cent of the sector's carbon emissions. In 2019 Ireland's Climate Action Plan conceded that the country was 'way off course' and vowed that by 2030 at least 70 per cent of its electricity would come from renewable sources, establishing the abandonment of peat fuel as national policy. The Bord had already announced in 2014 that it expected to stop extracting peat for fuel by 2030, but as climate breakdown has accelerated the company has been forced to scale back far more quickly than planned and has eliminated hundreds of jobs. The impact on the Midlands economy and working culture has already proved devastating, but even a radical transformation in energy policy will not undo the ecological damage that peat extraction has caused.

'Fifty per cent of Europe's raised bogs are in Ireland,' Whyte told me as we walked back to the car. 'We have a legal obligation to protect them, but less than 10 per cent are deemed worthy of conservation because they've all been impacted.' The Bord plans to 'rehabilitate' some 77,000 hectares of its depleted bogs – mainly by rewetting them and abandoning the sites to nature – but many conservationists think this is insufficient. In Whyte's view, 'Rehabilitation is not restoration, it's just stabilisation.' Those sites may cease to emit carbon, but the living bog will not return.

*

If Ireland's national consciousness can be sought in the matter of the country's

BOG ART

The influence of peat bogs on Irish culture is not limited to literature and is more present than ever in contemporary art. Bogs have been a permanent fixture in Irish landscape art ever since independence, thanks to painters such as Paul Henry and Maurice MacGonigal, but peat as a material entered the contemporary art scene with the German artist Joseph Beuys. After a stay in Ireland he created a sculpture in 1974 entitled *Irish Energy*, composed of two peat briquettes sandwiching a pound of butter. In 2000 the architect Tom de Paor used twenty-one tonnes of peat (in the form of 40,224 Bord na Móna peat briquettes) to build the first Irish pavilion at the Venice Biennale – an intense olfactory experience for visitors! After its five months on display the peat brought in from the Irish Midlands remained in the Giardini, intended as a gift of land for a city that is sinking into the sea. Even more ambitious was the project begun in 2002 by the sculptor Kevin O'Dwyer in collaboration with Bord na Móna. Sculpture in the Parklands in County Offaly is a twenty-hectare park on former bogland, where Irish and international artists are invited to create large-scale, site-specific sculptures linked to the landscape and the industrial heritage of the peatlands with the ultimate goal of exploring new possible futures for these watery environments that, in the words of Joseph Beuys, constitute 'the liveliest elements in the European landscape, not just from the point of view of flora, fauna, birds and animals, but as storing places of life, mystery and chemical change, preservers of ancient history'.

4000 BCE

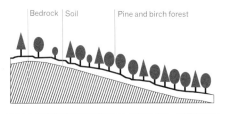

Bedrock | Soil | Pine and birch forest

2500 BCE
Land cleared for grazing and cultivation.

Leaching (where chemical substances in the soil are transported to lower strata by the action of percolating water)

500 BCE
Heather colonises the bare soil, turning it more acid. Undecomposed peat builds up on the higher ground.

Remaining trees choked by waterlogged peat

Agricultural activity moves to the lowlands

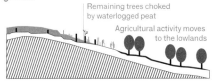

1000 CE
Peat builds up as the heather grows.

Bog

Agriculture expands in the lowlands

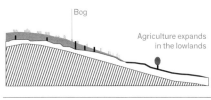

2000 CE

Peat cut for fuel

Conifer plantation

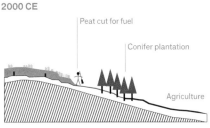

Agriculture

SOURCE: WWW.IRELANDSTORY.COM

terrain, it might be found in its bogs. Rainfall makes Ireland one of the boggiest countries on the planet, with peat covering 17 per cent of its land. With an extraordinary ability to preserve anything that might fall into their depths, the bogs are a museum of Ireland's deep past. Among the items dug up from the Bog of Allen: casked butter that has scarcely decayed since it was stowed centuries ago; two-millennia-old leather shoes, which look as if they were unlaced yesterday; a psalter, still legible after eight hundred years under ground. The Bord has a partnership with the National Museum of Ireland, whose archaeologists manage such finds, many of which have emerged in the course of the company's excavations.

For the poet Seamus Heaney – a kind of laureate of the bog – the landscape always had a 'strange assuaging effect ... with associations reaching back into early childhood'. The bog was liberty and community as well as labour. This ambiguous, borderless terrain – neither living nor dead, wet nor dry, public nor private – has never been politically neutral. Ireland's bogs were often viewed by city dwellers as fundamentally moribund: economic and cultural voids, the refuge of brigands, outcasts and hermits, synonymous with a semi-bestial peasantry – 'miserable and half-starved spectres', according to one 19th-century account. In folklore bogs are the lairs of the shape-shifting *púca* – an 1828 study of fairy mythology called them 'wicked-minded, black-looking, bad things' – while in Edna O'Brien's classic 1960 novel *The Country Girls* the protagonists are contemptuously dismissed as 'fresh from the bogs'. Throughout much of Irish history the bogs were also seen as impediments to economic progress. In 1731 an Act of

'If Ireland's national consciousness can be sought in the matter of the country's terrain, it might be found in its bogs. Rainfall makes Ireland one of the boggiest countries on the planet, with peat covering 17 per cent of its land.'

Parliament was passed to 'encourage the improvement of Barren and Waste Land, and Boggs, and Planting of Timber Trees and Orchards'. By the mid-19th century some thirty thousand hectares of bog had been reclaimed. Nevertheless, a geologist in Bram Stoker's 1890 gothic novel *The Snake's Pass*, quoting a former archbishop of Dublin, still complains, 'We live in an island almost infamous for bogs, and yet I do not remember that anyone has attempted much concerning them.' This was not to say that the bogs were irredeemable. 'We cure a bog both by surgical and medical process,' Stoker's geologist continues. 'We drain it so that its mechanical action as a sponge may be stopped, and we put in lime to kill the vital principle of its growth.' In theory, the process was straightforward: cutting networks of drainage ditches into the heart of a bog could dry out the peat, which could then be fertilised with lime, manured and ploughed. A 'worthless' bog was 'cured'.

But a bog is a product of climate and topography; it wants to be wet, just as a lake or a river does. Only through a tremendous, often uneconomical, investment of human energy could a bog be turned into a field of potatoes or a grazing meadow. Fuel, however, was another matter. Turf (the term given to peat cut for domestic use) was the very stuff of the bog, and if impoverished tenant farmers confined to such intransigent land had any advantage, it was the ready availability of free fuel.

Traditionally, once a bog had been drained, the living surface of plants and roots – the scraw – would be prised away and the exposed peat dug out using a spade with a wing on one edge called a *sleán*. Summer by summer, an escarpment of peat perhaps two metres high would advance from the bog's edges towards its centre, like an island being eroded by the sea. Once removed from the bog, the brick-sized sods of turf were spread out to drain for ten days or so, then stood up to dry in inward-tilting circles of five or six sods each – a process called footing. These assemblages of footed sods are still a familiar sight on Ireland's private bogs – of which there are hundreds – although these days the sods are formed from macerated peat, machine-excavated by contractors.

By the end of the 19th century bogs had come to function in British-ruled Ireland as a metaphor for a defiant national character. For advocates of British authority, reclaiming bogs was a way of subduing that character; for nationalists, the peatlands, as a potential domestic industrial resource, represented economic freedom. In 1946, after the obstruction of coal imports from Britain during the Second World War made the need for fuel self-sufficiency undeniable, an expansion of the Turf Development Board was announced, establishing the new semi-public company, Bord na Móna, Peat Board in English. An acerbic *Irish Times* columnist called the name 'an atrocious

'Bound up in peat's warmth, light and odour – even in its mechanically mined and machine-compressed form – were generations of positive associations: comfort, love, the family as a unit of the nation.'

neo-decadent Irish title', one that lent a phoney air of tradition to an entity 'set up for the purpose of incinerating large sections of your strictly limited Irish patrimony'. But incineration at such a scale demanded a workforce to match, a welcome development in a region of historically scant employment. 'Those who got jobs in Bord na Móna didn't have to emigrate,' one Bog of Allen resident told me. 'Lots of my relations went to England, America. The ones who were in Bord na Móna, they were staying at home.'

The post-war years saw the transition from sod peat – bricks cut by hand from the bog or formed in a mechanical extruder – to milled peat, a grainy, crumbly substance industrially scarified from a bog's surface. The milled peat is then either sent directly to power stations or ground into powder and compressed into oblong blocks to be sold as domestic fuel. Ask most people in Ireland what the Bord means to them, and they'll describe 12.5-kilogram 'bales' of moulded briquettes embossed with the letters BNM. Brittle as coal and bound in polypropylene strapping, they are widely available even now. Several Midlanders mentioned to me a TV commercial from 1986, preserved on YouTube. As the fiddle player John Sheahan of the Dubliners plays 'The Marino Waltz', a succession of blissful household vignettes unfold: a man removes his shoes and warms his feet by the fire; a little girl clutches her teddy bear and gazes contentedly into the flames; a woman embraces the lover she's been waiting for. Each two-second scene is illuminated by firelight – a special firelight, the kind endowed only by peat. Not a word is spoken. The briquette represents a timeless domestic idyll. Peat, the Bord recognised, was more than mere fuel. Bound up in its warmth, light and odour – even in its mechanically mined and machine-compressed form – were generations of positive associations: comfort, love, the family as a unit of the nation.

*

In 2003, near Croghan Hill about twenty kilometres north-west of Lullymore, police were alerted to the discovery of a body. The state pathologist determined that it belonged to a tall man in his late twenties who had been stabbed to death. His nipples had been sliced off and he had been beheaded. Gazing at what remained of his corpse, I could make out the whorls of his fingerprints, his manicured nails (he was not a working man) and the pores of his skin – skin that otherwise resembled an article of tanner's waste.

Old Croghan Man, as he is known, had been lying quietly in the peat since he was sacrificed more than two thousand years ago. In 2003 he was disturbed during the digging of a drain in a private bog; now he is on show in a vitrine at the National Museum of Ireland in Dublin. When I

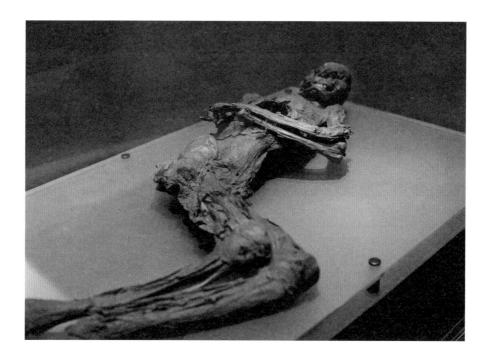

Gallagh Man is the name given to the preserved Iron Age human remains found in a bog in County Galway in 1821. Dating back to between 470 and 120 BCE, it appears he was a healthy male, 1.8 metres tall with dark-reddish hair and around twenty-five years of age at the time of his death. The presence of a noose – made of entwined willow – wrapped around his throat suggests that he was either strangled in a ritual sacrifice or executed.

visited, a couple of tourists joined me in the dim cubicle. One of them shuddered, slipped an iPad from her bag and took a photo. I couldn't help but feel there was something intrusive about our gawping. A notice informed us that:

Twisted hazel ropes known as withies were inserted through cuts made in the upper arms and may have been employed to fasten down the body to the bottom of a bog pool.

The bogs from which such bodies have been recovered often lie, as Croghan Hill does, on the boundaries between ancient kingdoms, no man's lands of uncertain sovereignty, where a life might be made to vanish.

'Why did they bury the bog bodies there?' asked Ray Stapleton, the manager of Lullymore Heritage and Discovery Park when I met him the following day. 'Because it wasn't tribal land. It was seen as an outlying area. The bogs have always been wild.' As its website explains, the park is 'the only attraction in Ireland offering a comprehensive insight into the Irish peatlands and the people living around [them]'. We were sitting in Stapleton's office, the cataract of rain on the roof so noisy that we had to raise our voices. He told me that he had been born in nearby Rathangan, a village established by Quakers that has been dominated by Bord na Móna since the 1940s. 'It was like the Wild West,' he said of the town's heyday, when hundreds of men from all over Ireland were brought to the Midlands to cut peat for the nation's new power stations. Stapleton grew up cutting turf each summer on his family's plot. 'I knew the bogs were different,' he said. 'You could find newts, dragonflies the size of your hand.'

The Heritage and Discovery Park was founded in 1993, partly to create local jobs following a series of cuts at the Bord. 'They had more modern machinery and didn't need as much manual labour,' Stapleton told me. The park's exhibition, with its bearded Neolithic mannequins and dioramas, introduces the natural and industrial history of Lullymore while, beyond the café and miniature golf course, visitors can follow a 'biodiversity boardwalk' to a flooded cutaway bog. 'What we've done is let the water back in,' Stapleton said. 'You just let nature take it back.'

He conceded that the legacy of the Bord's activity in the region was environmental ruin – the peat was largely gone and would take centuries to return – but maintained that the company extracted something more than jobs or energy from the bogs. 'That was us saying we're an industrial country, a modern country; we're able to provide out of our own resources – we don't need British coal.'

Most of the park's overseas visitors are German, which Stapleton attributes to their own affinity for peatland (technology pioneered on German bogs is still used by the Bord). British tourists have dropped off since Brexit and few Americans venture so far from the established sightseeing trails. He admitted

that it's a difficult sell. 'You're not going to the castle, you're not going to the Wild Atlantic Way, you're not going to the Cliffs of Moher, you're not going to Kilkenny ... You're going to the bog.'

When the Bord's last bog closes, Stapleton would like to see the greater part of the Bog of Allen rewetted, allowed to return to wildness and promoted as a green-tourism destination, a kind of Irish safari park. 'I often wonder what would it be like if we hadn't had to use our peat. I would love to have seen it when it was twenty feet up like a big cloak. That's what the poet Matthew Farrell said; he said the bog was like a cloak, surrounding Lullymore, protecting it.'

Later that week I read Farrell's 1860 poem 'Lullymore'. It's partly a wheedling encomium to Lullymore's landlord, William Murphy, but also an earnest, if sub-Wordsworthian, celebration of the Inland Isle's girding bog:

> Its texture of the richest brown,
> Set here and there with tufts of down,
> Embroid'rd o'er with heath bell trees
> And these bespangled o'er with bees
> With silky folds of mossy beds,
> Like pillows made for angels' heads,
> With mirror lakes divided through,
> Where countless stars reflect their hue.

*

Liberty Hall, the Dublin headquarters of the Services, Industrial, Professional and Technical Union (SIPTU), is a sixteen-storey tower block on the north bank of the River Liffey. Hand-painted on a metal shutter covering a ground-floor window are the words of James Connolly, the union leader who helped orchestrate the 1916 Easter Rising: 'The Irish people will only be free when they own everything from the plough to the stars.' I was there

"'It's like Guinness,' Connolly explained. "I've never heard of anyone who drank their first pint of Guinness and thought it was lovely. But if you go to any pub in the country, you'll see twelve old men at the bar, and you'll probably see twelve pints of Guinness. It's an acquired taste.'"

to meet Willie Noone, SIPTU's energy-sector organiser and a critic of how Bord na Móna and the government have managed the termination of the peat industry.

'Years ago people were put off the land by the English,' he told me, in a conference room overlooking the river, 'and it's built into the psyche that if you have land, you protect it.' As we talked his phone throbbed sporadically with incoming emails and texts – he was participating in a climate-crisis debate that night on RTÉ, Ireland's national broadcaster. A Midlands native, Noone also grew up hand-cutting turf on his family's bog. 'When I was young I hated it, because it was seen as a chore, something you had to do – it was dusty, it was dirty, you'd rather be off doing something else.' But having returned to the Midlands after stints living in England and Australia, he is one of the few people who still cut and dry peat for their own hearth. 'It's like Guinness,' he explained. 'I've never heard of anyone who drank their first pint of Guinness and thought it was lovely. But if you go to any pub in the country, you'll see twelve old men at the bar, and you'll probably see twelve pints of Guinness. It's an acquired taste.'

The Midlands has tended to be viewed as peripheral, despite its proximity to the capital, but the region was transformed

entirely in the 1940s by the establishment of the Bord. 'These weren't ordinary jobs,' said Noone. 'These were good jobs, real jobs, pensionable jobs, jobs for life, skilled jobs.' The development of large-scale peat extraction had the dual benefit of strengthening Ireland's energy security and summoning thousands of jobs out of soil that historically had almost no economic value. Much of the Midlands still consists of small farms eking out an existence from land that – precisely because of its peat – remains marginal.

Peat extraction, like farm work, is seasonal, mostly taking place between July and September when drier weather allows machines to access the bogs and the milled peat to dry. Most Bord contracts are for ten months a year or less and permit a good deal of flexibility. 'That actually dovetailed in with the way of life in the Midlands,' Noone said. Bog work allowed Midlands farmers to earn a regular salary while continuing to maintain their own farms. 'Between the two of them you had a good living. You could look after your mum and dad. You could send your kids to college.' In other words, employment with the Bord offered a solution to the poverty and isolation that had been ingrained in the Midlands for generations while keeping the population on the land. With the end of peat extraction, said Noone, 'all those farms go back to being uneconomical'.

A peat bog in Connemara, County Galway.

In late 2018 the Bord announced that it was seeking to dismiss up to 430 of its 2,200 employees in a voluntary redundancy programme. A year later it was announced that two of Ireland's three remaining peat-burning power stations would close at the end of 2020 as part of what the government called an 'accelerated exit from peat' that would see two million fewer 'Lullymore' burned each year. By then many employees had already taken voluntary redundancy packages: the Bord paid out almost $46 million in voluntary redundancy compensation in 2018 alone. The Bord also established a 'just-transition fund' of $12 million for retraining the newly unemployed; but for most of the company's workers, whose average age is fifty-six, it was too late to change careers. 'The problem with the Midlands is that it's all bogland,' said Noone, 'and there's not too many things you can do in bogland.' (In spring 2020 a further 230 Bord employees were 'temporarily let go' because of the Covid-19 crisis.)

With demand for briquettes also declining, Noone estimated that about seven hundred jobs had been lost so far and believed more would follow. Given the millions of tonnes of milled peat already stockpiled on the bogs and the uncertainty surrounding the remaining power station's future, most of the Bord's land is now falling silent. The machinery is being sold off or scrapped, and the degraded bogs will be transformed into wind farms or reclaimed as wetlands

*

Rain was falling heavily upon the Bog of Allen. I stood alongside Michael Kearney, a former Bord na Móna employee, at the edge of a desert of black. In front of us, parallel runways of exposed peat fifteen metres wide extended more than a kilometre into the hazy distance. Each strip was separated from its neighbour by a drainage ditch about two metres deep, its bottom bright with water. Running along the edge of every tenth bay was an embankment of stockpiled peat three metres high. People often describe the process of removing peat from a bog as 'harvesting', but although a bog may look like a field ready for sowing on Google Earth, up close the process resembles harvesting about as much as an array of wind turbines resembles a farm. It's more like open-pit mining. Still, looking out at the black expanse, Kearney had the air of one admiring a garden tended over a lifetime. When I suggested I grab my umbrella from his car, he suppressed a smile. 'You wouldn't see many umbrellas on the bog.'

This was Ballydermot Bog, which Kearney managed for the Bord for twenty years before he retired in mid-2018. A cutaway bog like Ballydermot needs to be closely monitored. It may be dead, but it is mutable and moody. Its nature can change from hour to hour, and the amount of peat it yields on any given day can differ wildly from that of neighbouring bogs.

A bog manager's enemies are water and fire. Heavy rain makes a bog too soft to be worked safely – it can take days to recover sunken machinery. Bog men still talk about 2012, the worst year in

THE PLOUGHING

Enthusiasts describe it as the oldest profession in the world – although that epithet is perhaps more commonly applied to another, very different form of employment. Working the land with a plough was fundamental for the development of agriculture and the human species but also has its own sporting offshoot: the ploughing championships, which have been held since the first half of the 19th century. These competitions measure the regularity of the furrows as well as the care, speed and depth of the ploughing. Age is no barrier, nor do you need an athletic physique – one of the most recent British championships was won by an 82-year-old, while the English champion, Mick Chappell, revealed the secret to his success was drinking five pints of beer the night before the final. Ireland is regarded as the homeland of the competition, and 'the Ploughing', its national championship, is even said to be the world's largest outdoor event, so it's no surprise that local politicians like to be spotted there in front of the TV cameras while Dubliners see it as an excuse for a trip out. The record-breaking events of recent years attracted almost 300,000 people and 1,700 exhibitors over three days, as it is also a major trade fair for the sector, a place to meet the manufacturers of agricultural machinery, even though people are particularly drawn to the vintage competition using horses rather than tractors. The first event in 1931 was held in a field of just 10.5 hectares, whereas these days they compete on 283 hectares of land.

'A cutaway bog like Ballydermot needs to be closely monitored. It may be dead, but it is mutable and moody. Its nature can change from hour to hour.'

the Bord's history, when the summer rains were so intense that by winter the power stations were close to exhausting their reserves. 'If we'd had another year like 2012 the power stations would have closed,' said Kearney. But the following summer turned out to be a record-breaker: dry and hot month after month, putting the bogs at risk of catching fire. Blazes triggered by sparks from machinery or spontaneous combustion have caused millions of euros of damage to the Bord's bogs. For that reason, part of a manager's job is simply to watch. When a fire breaks out there is nothing to be done but drive a bulldozer on to the stockpile and attempt to smother the flames with more peat. 'A fire'd be gone out and after twenty minutes you'd see just a little wisp of smoke,' said Kearney. 'You could spend all night watching it.'

As we returned to the car the deluge gradually gave way to a fine, directionless drizzle: *brádán* in Irish, misty rain. We passed a comparatively pristine margin of uncut bog, a tussocked carpet of mosses, grasses and heather not unlike Lodge Bog. 'This is the way the bog was,' Kearney said without sentiment. Before Ballydermot was excavated in the 1940s, he reckoned, its surface would have been ten metres higher than it is today – the height of a two-storey building. 'We're actually down to the lack.'

'Lack', or 'lac', or 'lak' – nobody I asked was sure of the correct spelling – is a regional term for the ground under the peat, far below the natural organic surface of the earth, which thousands of years ago would have been the bed of the lake from which the bog developed. Perhaps the word derives from 'lake', but it appears in neither Irish nor English dictionaries. Looking back into the excavated void, the bog's floor of gravel and limestone exposed, I had a momentary sense of being on the bed of a drained ocean – the dark mass overhead crushing in its absence.

*

It was just a few minutes from Ballydermot Bog to Kearney's home in the village of Clonbulloge. We drove back through the rain – *clagarnach* now, a torrent – along the route he'd taken almost daily for twenty years. 'One of our managing directors actually worked his way up from working on the bog as a general operator,' he said. And now? I asked. 'They wouldn't know what a bog looks like.' A few years ago, Kearney said, the Bord hired a consulting firm to improve efficiency. 'We had to put a flowchart up in the office. One lad had worked for PricewaterhouseCoopers, the accountancy firm. We had to tell him what we did on the bog from start to finish, and he came back in six months' time to tell us how to do it better.' He uttered the final word with a certain dryness.

Kearney's home was a smart white terrace house on the village green. A sign read 'TIDY TOWNS BRONZE-MEDAL WINNER'. As we entered I apologised to

Josephine, Michael's wife, for dripping water on the floor. 'As if we aren't used to that,' she said, leading me through to the kitchen. By the door to the back yard, brick-sized sods of dried peat were stacked against the kitchen counter. This same peat was blazing in the kitchen stove, and there was more stored in the shed, and more still – twenty tonnes, to last the winter – in another outbuilding.

'You'll have a slice of toast,' she said, dropping bread into the toaster. She left us alone for a moment, returning with a framed black-and-white photo of a handsome, smiling middle-aged couple on a peat bog. The woman was seated on a bench cut into a cliff face of peat. In front of her was a folding table on which stood a tin kettle and a jar of Bovril. The man, on top of the uncut bog behind her, was clutching a *sleán*. 'Daddy and Mammy on the bog,' said Josephine fondly.

Nobody ever believed the peat was depthless or that its removal at an industrial scale was anything less than violence done to the land and the country's 'strictly limited Irish patrimony', but even despoliation can look like an act of largesse in certain circumstances. If there is fatalism among the Bord's workers now, it's only because they know that the company's *raison d'être* has never been anything but provisional. The 'lack' was always there, waiting to be exposed. ✒

An Ocean of Wisdom

Traces of Ireland's once-flourishing fishing and maritime past, a way of life now in desperate decline as the foreign supertrawlers that ply the country's waters have taken over, can be found in the Irish language. Manchán Magan travels to the *Gaeltachtaí* to find local words and phrases that express aspects of the sea, weather and coastal life with extraordinary levels of nuance, traces not just of a disappearing world but also of a shared experience that it is vital to preserve.

MANCHÁN MAGAN

The village of Cill Éinne (Killeany) on Inis Mór (Inishmore), the largest of the three main Aran Islands in Galway Bay on the west coast of Ireland.

You cannot understand Ireland without understanding its relationship with the Irish language, and you cannot understand the Irish language without understanding the coastline where the last remaining Irish-speaking communities are still clinging on. So let's start with the coast. As an island, Ireland has no shortage of it; it coils and corrugates in and out like a chainsaw blade, having been carved and eroded by the roiling Atlantic Ocean and the winter storms that get whipped up on the four-thousand-kilometre expanse between us and North America.

While Ireland's eastern and southern shores are relatively sheltered by Britain and France and are thus not too eroded, the west coast is an endless fractal geometry of jagged inlets, headlands, craggy outposts, stacks and sea caves. I ought to be able to provide its overall length, but in Ireland facts about straightforward things such as these are often not that straightforward. Reality can be a shifting concept, depending on one's standpoint. The Irish government's Marine Institute cites 7,711 kilometres as the length of our coastline, while Ordnance Survey Ireland (the official mapping agency) claim it is closer to 3,171 kilometres. *The World Factbook* produced by the CIA gives a length of 1,448 kilometres, while the World Resources Institute, using data from the US Defense Mapping Agency, suggests 6,347 kilometres. And that's not even getting into the issue of whether the Northern Irish coastline should be included as part of Ireland or the United Kingdom. The fact is that the island is so jaggedly toothed that no one can quite agree how to measure it.

I could tell you that Atlantic storms have carved out some of the highest sea cliffs in Europe, but again that's debatable. The Slieve League Cliffs in County Donegal rise 598 metres above the ocean, making them nearly three times higher than the famous Cliffs of Moher in County Clare but not quite as high the Croaghaun Cliffs on Achill Island in County Mayo, which, at 687 metres, are Europe's second highest. What they all have in common is that they are in the most exposed, weather-ravaged areas of the island, places where elemental forces wreak the most havoc on daily life.

What we do know for certain is that 40 per cent of Irish people live within

MANCHÁN MAGAN is an Irish writer, documentary filmmaker and presenter of *The Almanac of Ireland* podcast on RTÉ Radio 1. He is the author of travel books and, with his brother Ruán, has made dozens of documentaries in the *Global Nomad* series as well as two series of *No Béarla*, in which he attempts to get by in Ireland speaking only in Irish. His books *Thirty-Two Words for Field: Lost Words of the Irish Landscape* (Gill Books, 2020) and *Tree Dogs, Banshee Fingers and Other Irish Words for Nature* (Gill Books, 2021) both explore the richness of the Irish language and reflect on the ways of life that are disappearing as the language becomes increasingly marginalised.

'We were poor at the time and needed the investment that Europe was offering. Now, as we look back, it's a matter of shame for us and anger, too.'

five kilometres of the coastline and that these settlements tend to be along the tamer eastern and southern coasts. We also know that we depended on the sea for our survival and for trade and recreation since settlers first arrived after the last ice age until recent decades when international flights and global trade upended the old world order.

We still have one of the largest seabed territories in Europe, encompassing an area ten times our land area, but that's a sensitive issue as we sold off the fishing rights to it when we joined the European Community in 1973. We were poor at the time and needed the investment that Europe was offering. Now, as we look back, it's a matter of shame for us and anger, too, especially when we look out at the supertrawlers from other countries and continents siphoning up the resources from our seas while our coastal fishing communities wither and die. The total allowable catch for Ireland in 2020 was just 195,000 tonnes, which equates to a financial return of €275 million ($320 million).

'I look at the pier in Dingle town, and all I see are huge boats from Spain and Portugal landing their fish and sending it straight off home,' says Seáinín Mac Eoin, a fisherman from Baile na nGall, County Kerry. 'There're twenty forty-foot containers a week being shipped out of there by foreign-owned vessels. We gave away our quota and never developed a fishing industry at home. Now the seas are practically fished out.'

John Bhaba Jeaic Ó Chonghaola, a fisherman from 320 kilometres further north

in Leitir Mealláin (Lettermullen), County Galway, agrees. 'Fishing has never been as bad as it is now. We haven't caught a single mackerel here in two years. Long ago an hour of fishing mackerel from a *currach* [a traditional canoe-type boat] would yield five or six nets full of them, but there are no mackerel left now. They've been taken by the big boats, out beyond. The supertrawlers.'

The land along the west coast is very different from that in the east and south of Ireland, too. It's wetter and more exposed and so has degraded more. Peatland began to form once the first Neolithic settlers felled the covering of trees that kept the thin layer of soil in place, and soon the land turned acidic and waterlogged. It could only ever offer subsistence living, and since then life has been a struggle. This was a key cause of the area's poverty as well as its isolation and the fewer railways and roads that exist in liminal, wilder places.

It was these factors that enabled the Irish language to survive here while it died out or was eradicated elsewhere. The areas where it is still spoken are known as *Gaeltachtaí*, which means Irish-speaking areas. If you think of Ireland as being the shape of a teddy bear, the Donegal Gaeltacht is where its head should be in the northwest, the Connemara Gaeltacht is in the location of its belly in the west and the Corca Dhuibhne Gaeltacht is at its toes in the south-west.

There are a few other tiny *Gaeltachtaí* along the west coast, but these are the three principal ones, with their own

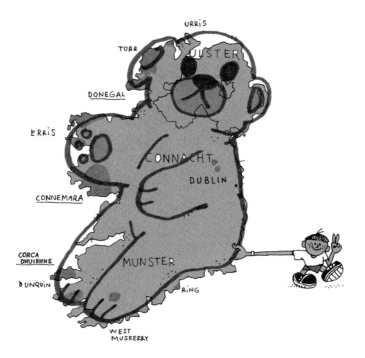

Irish-language development offices, Irish-language radio station and Irish-language television production companies. In total they have about 96,000 inhabitants, although over a third don't speak Irish and only a fraction use it daily. Each *Gaeltacht* has its own specific dialect, which were believed to be mutually unintelligible until a *Gaeltacht* radio station was set up the 1970s and people became more familiar with each other's dialects. Still today, though, there are marked differences between them, and it can be hard at times to understand people from a different *Gaeltacht*.

I should explain that the Irish language (also known as Gaelic or *An Ghaeilge*) is not in any way a dialect of English. Rather, it's an ancient and remarkably well-preserved strain of the original Indo-European language that moved across Europe from a region around the border with Asia many thousands of years ago. It has been spoken on the island for at least two thousand years and possibly up to three thousand years in some form and has managed to preserve many of its Old Irish and earlier Celtic forms (which, as it happens, are also still intact in Hindi).

Like other old tongues (Sanskrit, Hebrew, Sumerian) the Irish language has unique ways of expressing things that can be bamboozling to us now – one example of which is that Irish regards the unseen world as being just as real as the seen, and this is evident in many of the phrases, metaphors and colloquial expressions that make up daily speech. So the word *ceantar*, for instance, means place, region or locality, while *alltar* is its opposite, the other realm, the netherworld. They exist simultaneously in all places at all times. Our physical bodies occupy the *ceantar*, but our minds can easily slip into the *alltar*. Only a thin veil separates the two realms, and there were always those who could pass from one to the other, as is demonstrated by the word *púicín*, which refers to a supernatural covering that allows otherworldly beings to appear unseen in this reality. (It can also mean a blindfold, a goat's muzzle or a tin visor placed over a thieving cow's eyes.)

The marginalisation of the language to the poorest, most exposed and isolated regions should be no surprise to anybody familiar with the fate of minority cultures that are not actively fixated upon maximising the extraction of local resources and the endless expansion of personal wealth. All over the world such people are branded as backward or even barbaric. Anything of value they own is taken from them, and they are pushed to the margins, to wasteland that is of little value to anyone else. This is precisely what has happened to the Irish language. It has been forced ever westwards into the most disadvantaged areas, and currently our *Gaeltacht* regions stretch along 25 per cent of the coastline.

The largest city in the west of Ireland, Galway, is also the one in which the language is still most evident, although, to be fair, its presence is fairly minimal today. Yet you are still more likely to hear Irish there than in any other city. It's a coastal city that derives much of its income, like so much of the west coast, from tourism. It was once prosperous – as was its sister city Cork in the south-west – with wealth built upon international trade in butter, grain and salted fish to the ports of major Catholic cities in Spain, France and Belgium. But that all died out in the 18th and 19th centuries when Britain tightened its stranglehold on Ireland and deprived the Catholic chiefs and lords of their wealth and freedom. Both cities fell into a decline that wasn't reversed until tourism and the relocation of American tech and pharmaceutical production facilities helped revitalise them in recent decades.

MORE THAN JUST A ROCK

In a far-flung location in the middle of the Atlantic, around 160 nautical miles west of Scotland's St Kilda Islands and 230 north-west of Ireland's Donegal coast, stands Rockall, a rock measuring twenty-seven metres across and around twenty-five metres high. The vertiginous cliffs of this granite pyramid – which emerged over fifty million years ago and was mapped for the first time in the 16th century – are streaked with white from slippery guano. It is certainly no place for human habitation, but the real prize relates to what lies below: fish and oil. For decades its waters have been fished by Irish boats out of the port of Killybegs, helping to make it the Emerald Isle's largest fishing port, but a territorial dispute that has never been settled was further aggravated as soon as Brexit came into force, when an Irish boat was stopped by a Scottish patrol vessel. The UK has claimed sovereignty since a 1955 expedition, which was billed as an anti-Soviet mission, and in 1972 Rockall was annexed to the Scottish island of Harris. Other nations, in particular 'neighbouring' states – Ireland, Iceland and the Faroe Islands (Denmark) – have never recognised this unilateral move and refer to the international law of the sea, according to which rocks or small islands that cannot sustain human habitation or economic life of their own have no right to an exclusive economic zone. To get around this a couple of British adventurers have attempted to live there for brief periods, the record being a stay of forty-two days. The record-holder, Nick Hancock, also led the first tourist cruise in 2020; for a fee of $2,000 a head, visitors could spend twenty minutes on the disputed rock.

'In each county, and even on isolated promontories, peninsulas and islands within counties, I was offered an abundance of highly specific words that revealed particular aspects of the marine ecosystems, weather patterns, fishing practices and sailing techniques in those areas.'

In 2020 Galway was chosen as a European Capital of Culture, and I undertook a project as part of this to collect the sea words and coastal terms that still survive among the Irish-speaking fishermen and folklorists along the coastline of County Galway and stretching northwards from there to include Irish-speaking areas in the counties of Mayo and Donegal. The project and the journey along the sea roads and into remote coastal communities was revelatory in so many respects. I found the abundance of words to describe every conceivable element of sea life to be staggering. Hundreds of terms were offered to me for different types of waves, winds, seaweeds, shellfish and fishing conditions. The sheer specificity of some – such as *boilgeadán*, a young coalfish (*Pollachius virens*: coley/pollock) about thirteen centimetres in length, or *luiseag,* the back of a fish hook that is gripped to remove the hook from a fish's mouth – is bewildering to us who are now disassociated from this great storehouse of accumulated wisdom. It was proof of just how wide, deep and nuanced our forebears' understanding of the resources along our coastline was and their intimacy with coastal ecosystems and sea knowledge after millennia of accumulating and sharing knowledge within communities.

In each county, and even on isolated promontories, peninsulas and islands within counties, I was offered an abundance of highly specific words that revealed particular aspects of the marine ecosystems, weather patterns, fishing practices and sailing techniques in those areas – as well, of course, as highlighting the diverse beauty of the natural world. So, for example, *muirleadh*, according to sea folklorist Cormac Gillespie of An Bun Beag, County Donegal, is a word for when 'fishermen would chew on little crabs and then spit them out over the gunnel of the boat to attract fish. The fish would move in. Blood lust would take over.' He also has a word for forecasting bad weather, *buailteog*. 'If you look up at the sun sometimes you see a rainbow around it or a ray on the far side, and that is the *buailteog*. If it is open on one side and not complete, that's the side the bad weather will come from.'

Micí Whiting in Machaire Rabhartaigh, County Donegal, taught me the word *crom'ubhán*, 'a long pole with a hook on it, and you stick it into an *aicí* to pull out the lobster or crab. You'd have to be very quick to get him.' He went on to explain that an *aicí* is a hole in which a lobster hides. He also told me about a *léamhadóir*, which is the term for a man who watched for signs of herring shoals and who would then light a piece of paper and throw it on to the water so that his crew could make a ring around the shoal with their nets.

But what I also came to realise was

THE PASSENGER   Manchán Magan

John Bhaba Jeaic Ó Chonghaola, photographed in Leitir Mealláin (Lettermullen), County Galway.

The Tigh Mholly pub in Connemara, one of the few remaining strongholds of the Irish language, part of the Galway Gaeltacht, which is Ireland's largest Gaelic-speaking area. The pub's name is written in the Gaelic script.

something that I had never fully appreciated before, despite having made television documentaries, written books and performed plays about the Irish language for more than three decades, and that was something Pádhraic S. Ó Murchú from the fishing community of Leithinis an Mhuirthead in County Mayo said to me, 'Beatha teanga í a labhairt' ('The life of a language is the speaking of it'). It was he who first introduced me to the concept of stopóg, 'a grazing pasture for lobsters. The rays of the sun reach down to where it's sheltered and there's an abundance of small shellfish and plankton that he can live off. Mussels of all sorts grow there, too.' He differentiated it from a breaclach, which describes a sandier, stonier area of seabed.

All of these sea words are connected to very specific ways of fishing, of gathering seaweed, of sailing or collecting shellfish that have gradually been outlawed or made unviable by EU and government policy over the last forty years. 'The last remaining fishermen here wouldn't know what a stopóg or a breaclach were any more,' says Ó Murchú. 'None of the old men who knew these terms are still fishing. They had to give up as there's nothing left here.'

He reminisces about when there were fish all year round: herring and mackerel in autumn; white fish like coalfish in early spring; then lobster from April through to October. 'People used to leave from here with donkey cartloads of fish every Saturday morning to sell at the market almost year round. But that all fell apart as the seas were fished out by bigger boats. There's barely half a dozen boats still fishing on the peninsula where there used to be sixty or more.'

John Bhaba Jeaic Ó Chonghaola in Leitir Meallláin, 170 kilometres south of Leithinis an Mhuirthead, agrees. 'The sea here was full of salmon when I started fishing. You'd see them rising in the air the whole time. You never see that now. There's no salmon left anywhere along the coast. All that's left now are a few shellfish, but the crabs are almost gone and the lobsters are getting evermore scarce. I haven't put out any pots this year because the lads who are out fishing aren't catching anything.'

The Irish state didn't just commit one heinous act of betrayal upon the fishing communities by sacrificing them on the altar of progress to achieve EEC membership in 1973, they have continued ever since then to make life harder for the few small-scale fishermen in the Gaeltachtaí who have managed to keep on going despite the constraints of a tiny allowable fishing quota. They made a pragmatic decision to focus their resources on the few larger industrial fishing vessels out of the major ports of Killybegs and Castletownbere, knowing that without state support the fishermen in the Irish-speaking communities couldn't compete and that fishing would die there. These few big players now control an industry worth approximately €700 million ($810 million) a year and which provides around eleven thousand jobs. Total seafood exports in 2019 were worth €577 million ($670 million).

'There are now only thirty big boats left working the coastline, and they believe they have a right to take 90 per cent of the mackerel that swim there,' says Seáinín Mac Eoin in Baile na Gall, 'whereas the likes of me, whose father and grandfather were fishing mackerel on lines for generations, are forced to give up. A few rich men control all the shots.'

It seems the state actively decided to allow small-scale fishing to die out. Was

Above: A view of the cliffs close
to the prehistoric fortification of Dún
Aonghasa on the south side of Inis
Mór (Inishmore).
Right: A trawler in Rossaveal,
Connemara, County Galway.

Above: A pub sign in the Gaelic script.
Left: Michael Concannon and Patrick Maher look out over the fields and dry-stone walls of Inis Meáin (Inishmaan), the second largest of the Aran Islands.

it so that the *Gaeltachtaí* (which are often looked upon as akin to 'native reservations' and somehow backward and expensive to administer) would wither further?

'All hope is now gone for small fishermen like me in *Gaeltacht* areas,' says Mac Eoin. 'We're left scratching the bottom of the barrel trying to eke out a living. There's nothing really left to fish. Crabs used to be so numerous that we were driven demented with them. They were everywhere. Now they are gone. Fished out. The only thing that's left are a few lobsters in a season that lasts about eight weeks. Salmon fishing has been closed since 2006. When that was still being practised it took the pressure off the crab and the lobsters. They are now talking about banning crayfish netting in the next year or so and paying fishermen to stay at home. Meanwhile the foreign supertrawlers will continue to hoover up what's left.'

Fishermen find themselves with no option but to sell their boats and to move to cities in the *Galltacht* (English-speaking area) or to emigrate to Australia, America or Britain. With the departure of each individual the death of the *Gaeltacht* comes closer, as another fund of words and lore and local knowledge is lost with them. One often hears tragic stories of these enforced emigrants turning up in hospitals abroad with dementia and being able only to remember their mother tongue and so being incapable of making themselves understood.

However, in contrast, with the decline of the *Gaeltachtaí* and the small-scale fishing industry along the western shore, there is one thing that is thriving: tourism. 'The government decided to focus on tourism at the expense of everything else,' says Mac Eoin. 'Nothing else mattered. Though we've no fish left locally to feed them. We need to get them from the big processing centres in Killybegs and Castletownbere.'

For every Irish speaker who leaves the region many outsiders arrive to build holiday cottages, tourism businesses and retirement homes, as it just so happens that the *Gaeltachtaí* are situated in the most picturesque parts of Ireland. The spectacular cliffs I referred to earlier, Slieve League Cliffs in County Donegal and the Croaghaun Cliffs in County Mayo, are both in or close to *Gaeltacht* areas, as are so many of the other major Irish tourist sites, such as the fort of Dún Aonghasa on the Aran Islands, which dates back to 1000 BCE, or the 6th-century monastic settlement of Skellig Michael, which clings precariously to an embattled sea rock.

The dramatic rocky promontories, wild, churning waters and ferocious gales that made the land so inhospitable to live in, especially through the harsh winters, are what make it so attractive to summer visitors. In fact, one of Ireland's most successful recent government initiatives has been the Wild Atlantic Way, a 2,500-kilometre coastal driving route through a wind-blown, sea-washed landscape in the nine western counties, stretching from County Donegal's Inishowen Peninsula in Ulster to Kinsale Harbour, County Cork, in Munster. It passes directly through all the major *Gaeltachtaí* in the counties of Donegal, Mayo, Galway, Kerry and Cork, but tourists driving along it are rarely if ever encouraged to speak Irish or to respect the fact that they are in a unique linguistic and cultural region and that their presence, while helping the economy, is also diluting the spoken presence of Irish in the community.

What's needed is for Ireland to realise that we are the inheritors of a profound

Gone Fishing

In 2020 Manchán Magan set out along the coast roads of Mayo, Donegal, Connemara and Inishmore seeking out sea words, maritime terms and coastal customs. What he learned from the fisherman and inhabitants of these places can be found on his website (https://www.manchan.com) and a selection of the words he encountered have been collected in the book *Sea Tamagotchi* (RedFoxPress, 2020).

Mada doininne
[mada dɪnʲɪnʲɛ]:

Literally 'hounds of the storm', a dramatic way of describing a type of dark cloud that appears to be standing with its head held high.

Muirleadh
[mɪrʲlʲæɣ]:

When fishermen chew small crabs and spit them into the sea as bait to attract fish to the boat.

Caibleadh
[kabʲlʲæɣ]:

Spirit voices heard in the distance, particularly on calm nights at sea.

Racálach
[rakalax]:

Seaweed cast up on to the shore after a high tide or a gale, which is used for fertiliser.

Tine shionnaigh
[tʲɪnʲɛ çənaj]:

Phosphorescence in the ocean on dark, damp nights caused by a type of slime on seaweed and fish.

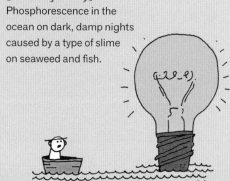

Neily Gallagher, a fisherman on the island of Árainn Mhór (Arranmore) off the coast of Donegal.

'The Irish language is gradually beginning to strengthen in urban centres away from the western shore, but the Irish learned from apps and books is a very different thing.'

linguistic legacy that describes and deciphers our world, our climate, our landscape and our daily reality (real and imagined) in a rich and nuanced way. If we want to understand the subtlety of our ecosystem and our psychology and to tap into the ways in which our ancestors survived and thrived in a sustainable way on the island over millennia we daren't cast off this language and all its inherited wisdom. There are specific insights within the language that we may need as we attempt to tackle climate change and address the social upheaval, coastal erosion and soil degradation that is increasingly part of our world.

Certainly the Irish language is gradually beginning to strengthen in urban centres away from the western shore, but the Irish learned from apps and books is a very different thing. It has few of the rich nuances that are an intrinsic but barely definable part of *Gaeltacht* life. And it tends to be the most nebulous, evocative, insightful and untranslatable words that are the first to be forgotten, such as *iarmhaireacht* ('the lonesomeness of cockcrow') or *súóg* ('a track left by tears on your cheek') – certainly you won't find those in any learners' textbook.

So what will happen to the Irish language? That, of course, is hard to predict, but what is clear is that the Irish people, like all people, need to find meaning in their lives again. This is a pivotal time all around the world; people are yearning for connection with something stable and greater than themselves. There is a growing awareness that we need to reconnect with nature and the heritage bestowed on us by our ancestors. In Ireland we can attempt to do this through the coloniser's language that was forced upon us by English oppression over centuries when they beat us for speaking our own language and outlawed it in the public sphere, but to do so may be harder and take longer.

We are fortunate in this country to still have our ancestral tongue alive and fortunate, too, that it's relatively strong compared with the majority of languages that are critically endangered. Every child learns Irish for at least a decade in school. If we choose to support the *Gaeltachtaí* and make serious efforts to keep our school-learned Irish alive we may see a cultural and psychological renaissance in which we would finally cast off the trauma of post-colonial oppression and find our ancient strength and our place in the world. Fortunately there is a new generation of young people keen to highlight the wealth of our language and heritage, not in any exclusive way but to show it as an example of the wisdom, creativity and beauty that is contained within all ancient cultures. More people are reconnecting to the natural word, too, and realising that our oceans and landscape need to be cared for. As Mac Eoin says, 'none of us realised how fragile the sea was until David Attenborough started his programme in the last few years. Now we are beginning to see where we went wrong and what we could do differently.'

The change is in motion. Like the sea, everything is in flux. ✒

SARA BAUME

Talismans

Taking her work on model cottages as a jumping-off point, the artist and writer Sara Baume reflects on the way her country's built environment has changed amid the legacy of the Celtic Tiger years and a new appreciation of traditional Irish architecture.

O f all the mass-produced souvenirs of Ireland – the cuddly sheep, the shamrock key chain, the Guinness candle, the plastic leprechaun, the harp-shaped fridge magnet – I harbour a particular affection for the Irish cottage figurine.

Typically, it's about as tall as a shot glass and no wider or longer than the palm of a hand. Painted the colours of thatch, whitewash and timber, it has a hipped roof, four low walls, two small front-facing windows and a half-door. There might be flower boxes on the windowsills, a stack of turf against the wall, a bumpy garden of rocks and grass, a winding path trailing off the edge; there might even be a tiny lever protruding from a gable that, when gently cranked, plays a plinky-plonky version of 'Danny Boy'.

Whenever I refer to the miniature cottage, I carelessly, repeatedly use the word 'figurine', even though I know it's technically incorrect; a figurine is most precisely an ornament depicting the human form. I use it involuntarily because it feels appropriate. There is something anthropomorphic about the cottage that other buildings lack – its heavy golden fringe and pale cheeks, its mouth hung slightly agog.

This summer I unearthed a photo-book called *Irish Cottages* by Walter Pfeiffer and Maura Shaffrey (Weidenfeld and Nicolson, 1990) from a cluttered stall in the weekly market of a coastal town close to where I live – a market that is in many ways symbolic of contemporary Ireland, swallowing the entire esplanade and peddling everything from fishing tackle, hardware and antiques to live ducklings, Indian spices and paper bowls of patatas bravas. The book is mostly composed of handsome photographs of cottages in unexpected variety; the introduction posits, compellingly, the idea of smallness as an architectural virtue. The first time I flicked through its pages I experienced a strange gush of nostalgia. The pictures in the book were familiar to me, and yet at the same time they were foreign.

Irish Cottages was published in 1990; fourteen years later, on 3 December 2004, the British writer and environmental activist Mark Lynas published a long article in the *Guardian* entitled 'The Concrete Isle'. 'Forget what you've seen in the tourist brochures,' he starts, setting the tone. 'Today's reality is altogether different. If you want a tamed landscape dotted with off-the-shelf mock-Georgian houses, congested with nose-to-tail traffic

Left: A miniature cottage on Inis Mór (Inishmore), the largest of the Aran Islands in Galway Bay on the west coast of Ireland.

SARA BAUME is an award-winning writer and artist who was raised and still lives in County Cork, Ireland. She has contributed to publications such as the *Irish Times*, the *Guardian* and *Granta* magazine. Her debut novel, *Spill Simmer Falter Wither* (Tramp Press, 2015, Ireland/ Mariner, 2016, USA/Windmill, 2018, UK) was shortlisted for the Costa First Novel Award, among others, and won the Geoffrey Faber Memorial Prize. Her second novel, *A Line Made by Walking* (Tramp Press, 2017 Ireland/Mariner, 2018, USA/Windmill, 2018, UK) was shortlisted for the Goldsmiths Prize in 2017, and her most recent title, the non-fiction *handiwork* (Tramp Press, 2020), was a finalist at the 2021 Rathbones Folio Prize. Her third novel, published in 2022, is *Seven Steeples*.

> 'The cottage is the dwelling indigenous to our built environment – a structure that grew out of the soil like a bizarre knoll.'

and suffused by an ugly suburban sprawl, then *céad míle fáilte* – welcome to Ireland.' What follows is a compelling denunciation of the Celtic Tiger; Lynas describes a natural landscape as well as multiple sites of archaeological significance plundered by poor government and a generalised shallowness of morality. Although he interviews representatives of both sides of the argument, it's the voices of the Tiger's dissenters that make the most impact. 'What is going on across the board in this country is immensely destructive,' says Frank McDonald, then environmental editor of the *Irish Times*. 'The level of housebuilding spells catastrophe for scenic landscapes and the countryside in general if it continues.'

Smallness, evidently, is an aesthetic principle that was committed to Ireland's past during the years of economic prosperity or, at least, confined to the domain of the souvenir.

I didn't read Lynas's article in the year it appeared. In 2004 I was at university in Dublin, and I didn't return to live in the parish where I'd grown up for another four years. By then it had conspicuously changed – an inordinate number of new houses had popped up, even a couple of little housing estates, and the volume of traffic passing through the crossroads outside my parents' house in the mornings and evenings had increased as a consequence, conjuring a soft and staggered sort of rush hour, flanked by cattle, barley and brambles. At first I was disgruntled about what I perceived to be a

defilement of the landscape of the idyll of my childhood – the hacking down of trees I'd once climbed and the concreting over of grassy hills I'd once rolled down. These new houses stood in dramatic contrast to the vernacular architecture and even to the bungalows that had dominated from the 1970s to the early 1990s. Everything about them was incongruous. They were huge; sometimes more than a dozen windows pocked the façade, and they were spangled with unnecessary appendages – turrets, mock-fanlights, asymmetrical dormers and expansive conservatories. In addition, the homeowners, wherever possible, had chosen to situate their new country houses at the ends of protracted driveways and behind tall metal gates that opened electronically, majestically, as their SUVs approached.

But in the months leading up to the economic bust of 2008 my disgruntlement softened into curiosity. I developed a habit of sneaking around the parish where I had grown up, taking photographs of the houses that were foreign to me. Later I made sketches of them, and later again I built miniature replicas out of miscellaneous scrap – rags, cardboard, timber offcuts, even straw. The idea was to draw a contrast between the grandiosity of the monster mansions and my choice of coarse, everyday materials – the intention being to invent an updated and deeply cynical souvenir.

'The Irish have never been an urban people by nature,' writes Marion McGarry in her book *The Irish Cottage: History,*

Culture and Design (Orpen, 2017). 'When we think of our major cities and towns they were variously founded by foreigners – Vikings or Anglo-Normans. To live in small groups in the rural countryside was part of Irish culture for generations.'

The cottage is the dwelling indigenous to our built environment – a structure that grew out of the soil like a bizarre knoll, a primordial rearrangement of rock and wood and straw. I can picture the apex of a chimney peeking up from the grass, followed by the ridge of the roof, the bristly trim, the stone walls and front-facing windows. It was composed of materials provided by the locality and designed in concord with the weather and environment, favouring level land and sheltered spots, facing away from the prevailing winds. And the Irish cottage licked substances out of nature to inflect itself with colour – lime wash making white, copper sulphate making pale blue, slag deposits of iron making different shades of yellow and brown.

In the decade and more since the economic bust I've continued to build miniature houses in some form or other, at times with purpose, although more often haphazardly. In the beginning each structure tended to be around the size of a doll's house and reasonably representational; over time they have come to be smaller and more abstract. For my recent series, entitled *Talismans*, each structure – like the Irish cottage souvenirs – is scarcely taller than a shot glass and roughly the length and width of the palm of my hand.

On the ground floor of the 'Country Life' exhibition at the National Museum of Ireland in County Mayo there is a reconstruction of the interior of a 19th-century cottage. In summer 2018 I made a pilgrimage there to meet McGarry

and to talk about indigenous architecture – or, perhaps, human behaviour.

'To understand Irish cottages is to understand this mindset of not standing out too much from the crowd,' McGarry writes, 'not showing off creature comforts, and not trying to elevate one's social status through the exhibition of a "taste" in architectural trends.' McGarry puts the cottage in context as a logical response to the modest needs of the people who lived off the land and sea – people who were poor, but only averagely so, and full of pride. The bungalow, for McGarry, represents a 'natural descendant' of the cottage in scale and shape, but she points out how it soon came to be embellished by 'arches, concrete balustrades and stone cladding' and to be situated prominently, brazenly on the landscape, whereas cottages had more usually been hidden down lanes or surrounded by trees.

This mindset of utmost humility has completely transformed over the decades.

'Western identity,' McGarry states, 'has become increasingly associated with "the individual" as opposed to the "herd" attitude of our ancestors. With this came the ambition to reflect individuality and educated taste in one's home.' In the *Guardian* article of 2004 one of Lynas's interviewees is Ian Lumley, a heritage officer with An Taisce – the National Trust for Ireland. Lumley describes the Irish mentality as 'inherently anti-regulation and anti-officialdom'. He suggests that 'one of the theories is that this goes back to British occupation, to dodging the constabulary, dodging the revenue, getting away from the landlord, hiding pigs under the bed, hiding chickens in the roof and so on'.

These two contradictory factors combined – our historically fractious

Sara Baume's installation for the 'Home: Being and Belonging in Contemporary Ireland' exhibition at the Glucksman Gallery, Cork, in 2021 presents one hundred small cottage-like objects made from moulded, carved and painted plaster.

The artist and writer Sara Baume on the beach
at Long Strand near Clonakilty, County Cork.

relationship with authority, in this instance levelled against regulations regarding the protection of environment and heritage, and our tendency to emulate the architecture of the old country houses of the Protestant Ascendancy of the late 17th to early 20th centuries – go some way towards explaining the proliferation of the monster mansions.

In the downstairs of the reconstructed cottage, McGarry showed me around the furniture and implements and explained the various meanings behind their arrangement.

In her book she describes how 'the fire was both physically and socially situated in the centre of the house'. Whereas European families routinely gathered around the kitchen table, the Irish would push all of their furniture back against the walls to surround the light and heat of the hearth.

In the reconstruction McGarry pointed out how most of the items owned by the cottage dwellers would have been sourced from natural materials – gorse was used as a brush to sweep the chimney, straw was woven to make chairs, dried cow-pats were burned on the fire and the wing of a goose was used as a feather duster.

And then there was iron, which served multiple purposes – it was strong, practical and fireproof, but it was also believed to protect against 'faery' activity. Iron nails would be inserted into the walls of the cottage, and horseshoes would be hung from a nail alongside the chimneys and windows and doors – any points at which the faery folk might be tempted to enter. A poker would be placed across a cradle to prevent the baby inside from being stolen.

Perhaps the feature that interests me most – and the piece of furniture whose form I am borrowing from to build a display for my series of figurines – is the dresser, which was 'primarily a decorative piece' and 'a point of pride'. If you couldn't afford a dresser, McGarry told me, some kind of simpler alternative would always be fashioned, sometimes even just a shelf. For many decades in Ireland strong pagan beliefs and rituals coexisted and even commingled with those of Roman Catholicism, and this is embodied by the 'holy shelf', which, McGarry explains, was 'traditionally reserved for the display of holy objects, statues and pictures, and lit with candles'. I am very attached to this idea that no matter how meagre a person's way of life it is essential to reserve a space for lining up those possessions considered to be most precious.

Talismans, as a completed installation, is a ten-metre-long horizon line of miniature houses, each carved from plaster to the rough scale of a cottage souvenir but in the style of a contemporary rural dwelling – large, asymmetrical and endowed with an abundance of unnecessary appendages. At the beginning of the line-up the structures are recognisably house-like, but as the line proceeds they become increasingly abstract, and by the end each structure looks more similar to a stack of toy blocks than any kind of home. The horizon line is supported by a narrow shelf running along a wall of timber strips painted in temperate, domestic shades of yellow and trimmed, positioned and pinned to echo the tongue-and-groove panelling of a traditional dresser.

This installation is my most purposeful series of house-like structures to date; from 2017 to 2018 I sat for four or five hours most evenings cradling these small structures – first carving and later assembling them, and later again painting and repainting them. As I worked I would listen to the radio, and it was only towards the end of the project that I realised how

For many years now housing has been central to Ireland's public debate. Investment in bricks and mortar has always been very popular on the island, and even before the Celtic Tiger boom Ireland had one of Europe's highest rates of property ownership, something that was further accelerated by easy access to credit that in time led to the real-estate bubble. The ensuing crisis caused prices to collapse for several years, offering enticing opportunities for big international property companies such as I•RES REIT or California-based Kennedy Wilson, who got their hands on thousands of apartments while also taking advantage of the low rate of taxation. In the ten years from 2004 the percentage of homeowners fell from 81.8 per cent to 68.6 in 2014. If investors have been able to celebrate the rebound in prices in recent years, housing has become a serious issue in Dublin. You only need to note that in 2020–1 the average cost of a home was nine times the average salary. While houses in the city are out of reach, the Irish countryside is dotted with brand-new buildings abandoned in the wake of the crisis. And then County Donegal is going through a nightmare all its own, with the walls of over five thousand houses crumbling because the cement used by the building supplier Cassidy Brothers had mica mixed into it. Rocked by the scandal, the firm admitted its responsibility although added in its defence that everything it did was within the law. The government is trying to help out the unfortunate owners of the crumbling homes but is not managing to keep up with the wave of compensation requests.

the national news stories that had dominated that twelve-month cycle concerned the worsening housing crisis.

It was a year of rising rents, rising house prices, rising homelessness – and I had spent it shaping talismans as if by this means I might interpret my anxieties about the extinction of landscapes and the scarcity of sustainable homes; as if these miniatures and the process of their making might symbolise an attempt to protect against the future as well as to preserve the past.

As Ireland has changed, the mass-produced souvenirs intended to characterise and commodify it have changed in response, becoming more innovative and ironic. They now extend to include bog-flavoured air freshener, little jars of liquid luck, turf craft kits and instant Irish accent mouth spray.

Today there is among Irish people a renewed appreciation for our vernacular architecture and a return to the concept of building a house with sensitivity to its surroundings, although it feels to me like these acts of contrition have come too late. The majority of traditional cottages have already crumbled back into the undergrowth they sprouted from – their charming faces washed grey and blank by weather and time.

'Because of its strength,' McGarry writes, 'the chimney wall is one of the best preserved parts of many abandoned and ruined cottages.' And so the feature that once formed the hub of a family's movement and noise and warmth is now all that remains, planted silently into the soil, silhouetted smokeless against the sky, scattered across the Irish countryside like the headstones of untended graves or the standing stones of an ancient era – the earliest of all marks made on the land by human hands. 🐦

Everything That Falls Must Also Rise

Colum McCann

To leave home but never forget: the New York-based writer Colum McCann reflects on the choice he and so many others made to emigrate, leaving their native country behind but carrying it in their hearts for ever.

69

Every time I return to my native land I begin, once again, to understand the function of memory. This is the land I once walked across, from Dublin to Galway, in a nine-day rainstorm. This is the land where, as a child from the uncomplicated suburbs, I began to recognise the heft of violence. This is the land where light plays with shadow, perhaps more than anywhere else on earth. Bogland, tenement, winding backroad, leaping river, squinting glance. The land of saints, scholars, schizophrenics.

We are built on the wounds and the mercies of the past: everywhere we are is everywhere we have once been. And if any country captures the agile contradictions of our 21st century, it is, for me, the Ireland that I have known and loved.

It is still stunning to me to realise this, but I left Ireland over three decades ago. Coming home – and although I live in New York, I still call Ireland 'home' – I find my ribcage prised open and my heart wrung out like an old dishrag. Gone is the tiny muddy path to my old school. Someone has built a glass tower on the patch of soil where we schoolkids used to fight. There's a superhighway going through the old football field. My secondary school is unrecognisably built up. Changed, changed, utterly changed. But nostalgia is dangerous, of course. There is no point in wearing ancient shoes: they are worn down and they pinch too hard and you're never going to get very far in them.

Returning to Ireland, I walk around in a body that tries to acknowledge the presence of the past and the intricate promise of the future.

COLUM MCCANN was born and raised in Dublin and now lives in New York. He is the author of seven novels and three short-story collections, for which he has received numerous awards – including the US National Book Award and the International Dublin Literary Award for *Let the Great World Spin* and an Oscar nomination for the screenplay of *Everything in This Country Must* – and his work has been published in over forty languages. His most recent novel, 2020's *Apeirogon* (Random House, USA/Bloomsbury, UK), was a *New York Times* bestseller.

The Ireland of my memory is, I believe, not just a romanticised thing, or certainly not *only* a romanticised thing. I lived it in the '6os, the '7os, the '8os. I walked it. I cycled it. Coast to coast. North to south. The mountains. The rivers. The seascape. The boglands. The rippling waters of Lough Neagh. The trees in Powerscourt, bent by the rigours of weather. The swallows curving over the cliffs along the Giant's Causeway, turning and returning, time and again. The valley of Glendalough where the light was, I honestly believe, more profound than any other light on earth.

I loved it, but I disliked it, too – the cloying dreaminess, the begrudgery, the lockdown mentality of the Catholic Church, the valleys of the squinting windows, the incessant gossip.

In 1986 I left it behind and went to the United States. It was supposed to be a short-term trip, but it ended up being, more or less now, a lifetime.

It strikes me that perhaps one of the reasons I left Ireland is because I did not want to forget its inherent beauty. It is in the nature of the emigrant to wound himself or herself in order to remember. We leave in order to recall what once was. It's like a sort of mental tattoo. We carry it with us no matter where we go, preserved in the deep synapses of our minds. It is there, and we can access it as it once was, unencumbered by the reality of the present. James Joyce once said that he had been so long out of Ireland that he could 'hear her voice in everything'.

So, at the age of twenty-one I took a bicycle across the United States. The trip took a year and a half. In the course of the journey I changed. I became more and more interested in the stories of others. I recognised that I was entering the vast democracy of storytelling, and I liked the idea of that landscape. What was the world made of but other people? I loved sitting and listening to them. I stayed in their houses, slept in their fields, sat at their dinner tables. I met all sorts of people: rich, poor, black, white, funny, sad, beautiful, tainted. I finished the journey coming across the Golden Gate Bridge in San Francisco, after eight thousand kilometres, knowing that there was a whole other world out there that I wanted to see.

I went to Texas for a couple of years, working with juvenile delinquents in a wilderness programme. I went to college for a couple of years. And then I got married and went to Japan. By the time I was thirty I was living in New York and trying to make a living as a fledgling writer. Some of what I wrote was about Ireland, but other books had nothing to do with the memory of the place at all.

I went home to Dublin once a year, mostly for Christmas. But I always left again. I was a person of two countries. I had my hands in the dark pockets of each.

And while I was away, Ireland had changed. But what else did I expect? The change was gradual and often good. Europe had lined our pockets. The poverty had been lessened. The potholes were filled. A renewed sense of health had returned to the country. My generation had been a generation of emigrants, but suddenly people my age were staying and putting down roots. Ireland became a little more fashionable, a bit more hip. It was a decent place to live. It wasn't a country living in the shadow of Britain any more. Our literature was changing. International publishers were buying Irish books. The world was interested in us. And we sat up and took notice not only of our country but ourselves.

Throughout the 1980s and '90s I enjoyed going home. I even contemplated returning for good, but I had begun to put a life down in New York. I was married, I had children.

And then, in the early 1990s all the way through to the mid-2000s, the Celtic Tiger began to purr and roar.

Something startling happened. The Republic of Ireland became a country so jauntily happy with itself that it seemed nothing could go wrong. Midas developed a brogue. Bankers bellied up the bar. Farmers put television screens in their tractor cabs. Taxi

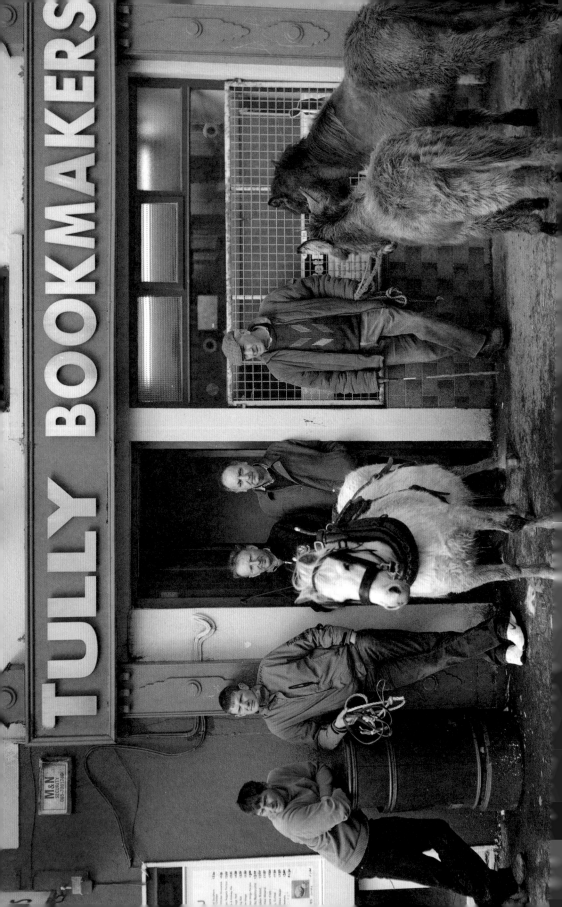

drivers became experts in hedge-fund investing. Every Tom, Dick and Paddy had a share in an apartment on the beach in Croatia. Highways were built through ancient burial sites like the Hill of Tara. The world seemed to breathe on the scent of money. Immigrants made a sort of Brooklyn out of inner-city Dublin.

By 2003 the Irish gross domestic product per capita outstripped everybody in Europe except Germany. Cranes swung like toy things across the skyline. Apartment buildings mushroomed into the countryside. All the number plates were new and up to date.

Coming home, I felt like an impostor. Streets had changed. Multi-lane highways had sprung up. I could not find my way from the airport. People sniggered at the American accent of my children. The country seemed arrogant and unstoppable. It was so much like the vanity of an adolescent: good hair, good teeth, goodbye. The party was on. I was too old and foreign to be invited. At the door I lingered for a little while. *Oh please fock off,* the hostess in her mid-Atlantic accent seemed to say, *and take your sentiment elsewhere.*

I felt my Irish voice disappearing. I found myself torn between anger at what was happening and an equivalent anger at my own apparent sentimentality, maybe even my complicity of silence. Each time I visited it became a more distant planet. Enlightened social legislation was dismantled. The political smiles were vapid and money-fed. The robber barons moved in. There was stunned submission to greed. A demolition of heritage. There was financial thuggery going on at every level of society: there was a beggar on O'Connell Street who sneered at the notion that he would get less than a euro dropped in his hat.

I hated it.

Everything that falls must also rise. So, if we accept the cynical, we must also accept at least the possibility of hope.

The other narrative that ran alongside the Celtic Tiger in the course of my absence from Ireland was that of the peace process in Northern Ireland. I had spent many of my boyhood summers up north on a farm in Derry, and I had seen, sometimes first hand, the devastation that war could inflict on a country: the bomb craters, the funerals, the hunger strikes, the blown-off horses' hooves dangling in the trees.

But in the early 1990s the remarkable began to happen and a peace process began to unfold. There was eight hundred years of arterial bitterness to confront. Incredibly – under the guidance of the US senator George Mitchell – a peace agreement was negotiated and ratified in 1998. It quivered at times, but it held. Gone were the random murders in the docklands of Derry. Gone were the young girls on the streets of the Shankill doused in tar and feathers for falling love with the wrong boy. Gone were the hand-held mirrors slid under cars to check for explosives. Gone were the women stumbling out of the supermarkets with bomb-blast blood dripping from their ears. Gone were the horses blown to bits for the sake of their regimental dress.

In the new century peace began to bring a new colour to Northern Ireland. Belfast felt like a city that has just run out into the fresh air. You could hear jazz coming from a tapas restaurant at the end of Botanic Avenue. The new Titanic Belfast museum spoke to the notion that even the heaviest things can be dredged up from the bottom of the sea. In the countryside the barbed wire was taken down from the checkpoints. Military radio towers were toppled. Slowly the schools were becoming desegregated, old alliances torn down. Immigrants arrived. New faces, new glances, new vistas. There were even Muslim city councillors who suffered the wrath of Catholics and Protestants alike. (There is an old joke that runs the streets of Belfast. A thug walks up to a man in the street and asks him if he is Catholic or Protestant. 'I'm Jewish,' he replies, thinking that his answer will save him. The thug steps even closer to him and says with a jaunty menace, 'Ach aye, but are you a Catholic Jew or a Protestant Jew?')

There are still, these days, issues of flags, riots, territorialism

in Northern Ireland. And marching season still manages to institutionalise old hatreds. But the province has, at its heart, changed dramatically. Returning to my mother's family farm in Garvagh, I feel myself charged and invigorated. What is this country unfolding at my feet? What possibility still lies here?

Is this another form of home?

It is the essence of human instinct to be able to hold opposing ideas at the exact same time. It is also a fundamental instinct to know that there is no absolute black, no absolute white and that most of what we encounter in life is grey.

Sure, the Celtic Tiger hammered the vision of my Ireland. The year 2008 slid a malevolent knife into the financial system. The economy began collapsing and then went into freefall. For eight years after the collapse there were hundreds of empty buildings on the outskirts of Dublin. Ghost towns in the countryside. The Irish pub was more or less disappearing: there were 'Closing Down' signs all across small villages. The scars of excess became tragic. The economy suffered. The people suffered.

But a certain sense of humility returned. It was obvious when I went back. It felt like I was returning to a place that was much more real. I didn't feel out of step any more. It was OK to still call it 'home'.

I realised then that Ireland would not leave me even if I had left it.

The sways continue. After such a terrible battering, the country started to recover once again around about 2015 or 2016. The economy got up off its feet. People seemed to shake off the concussion. The face of the country changed, too. Parts of Dublin looked more and more like Brooklyn. Immigrants came and changed the nature of who we were. Refugees, too. And, of course – as the economy recovered – the buildings continued to go up. Spectacular new bridges, theatres, office buildings. With it rose – for me at least – the sense of a whole new Ireland.

Today it's a country very much on the rise again, but it's not a slouching adolescent any more, it's more sophisticated, more alluring and more – dare I say it – middle aged.

Now, the more I return, the more I accept. This is, of course, a process of my own ageing, but I have – to my surprise – become far less nostalgic about the place. I have gone through enough cycles of coming and going that I know the sheer inevitability of change. I am not inured to sadness – parts of the west of Ireland look as if a dive-bomber has come in and sprayed cheap cottages all over the landscape – but it is easier for me to acknowledge the differences.

I go back, I walk around, I explore. I don't mind getting lost any more. There's a certain solace, in fact, in getting lost.

In Northern Ireland the peace process holds. It's shaky, but it holds. Brexit threw an enormous spanner in the works, but there are signs now that the distances are dissolving and that one day there will be no north, no south, just a proper Ireland to return to. If that happens – peacefully, of course – it may become one of the great stories of the 21st century.

A country is composed of its people far more than its land-scape. Let's face it. We're torturously poetic. We're unbearably self-conscious. We're awkwardly comic. We're wilfully ambig-uous. We'll answer a question with another question. We'll give you directions towards the exact place you don't want to go. We'll walk a hundred miles to receive a good insult. We're blasphe-mous. We're contrarian. We never forget a grudge. We address incomprehension. Our war songs are merry. Our love songs are sad. We have half-doors: we are neither in nor out. We make great fun of despair. And we're marvellous at spouting rubbish about ourselves. (*Mea culpa, mea culpa, mea maxima culpa.*) But we are also open to change. It is the eternal dream: to keep on becoming something new. The Irish have always had a great sense of humour, none more so than when their backs have been

against the wall. The one thing that has never been given up on, in the Irish psyche, is the presumption of hope – and indeed the presumption of home.

Joseph Brodsky says that you can't go back to the country that doesn't exist any more. It is true. But in a sense we return through our stories and our storytelling, which is a form of memory-making. Stories are what we are, what we are made of. This is, of course, true around the world – we are all stitched together by narrative, whether we be in Italy or South Africa or Belgium or Russia or Canada or Mexico – but I don't know if there's another place on this vast spinning rock where stories are so ambitiously told and received.

There's something fundamentally Irish about sitting down to tell a story. Maybe it's the rain that drives us indoors. Maybe it's the booze. Maybe it's the light that demands a sort of nuance. Maybe it's the character that looks for an argument – we are famously wedded to our grudges. Maybe it's the history of needing to stake a claim to a patch of land. Maybe it's our religious heritage that has damned us with guilt. Maybe it's because a story weaves the fabric of how we will be remembered, making us a part of for ever.

And there are still plenty of places where I can go back to the stories of my youth – where the light still falls just right on the silvery waters or where a stone wall snakes mysteriously through a field. There are still some country pubs where a fiddle will be broken out from under an overcoat later at night. And there is still the sense that life goes on, even in spite of the hardships.

A lot can be taken away from us, but not our memories or our stories. And not those places that can spark our memories either. This is what 'home' means. Home is a story.

And so I keep on returning. I arrive in Terminal 2 in Dublin Airport. I walk out through the high metallic-and-glass shine. I see all the immigrant faces looking upwards at the drizzle of rain. I drag my suitcase behind me. I rent a car. I consult the map to see where all the new highways lead. I think maybe I'll go north this time, to Strangford Lough or up around Donegal. I look left and right and I see myself, thirty-six years ago, walking through the landscape of memory. This, then, is what countries teach us. It's not a bad feeling, the ability to remember what we once were.

I am forced to realise that I have been out of Ireland for many years but, in fact, I have never left. She haunts me. Always has, always will. And maybe that's what leaving will do to you: it forces you to remain.🐦

At the Edge
of Two Unions:
Northern Ireland's
Causeway Coast

County Antrim looks out over the North Channel that separates Ireland from Great Britain. This is the 'narrow sea', which, post-Brexit, the EU and the UK agreed would be the point after which customs checks would be introduced to avoid reinstating a land border between Northern Ireland and the Republic and risk the collapse of the peace process. The BBC's former political editor in Northern Ireland introduces us to a region hanging in the balance with a foot in two unions, torn between fear and opportunity and with a widespread sense of having been abandoned.

MARK DEVENPORT

The ruined medieval Dunluce Castle is the seat of Clan McDonnell. Located on a basalt outcrop in County Antrim, between Portballintrae and Portrush, it can be accessed by a bridge that connects it to the mainland.

85

When you visit the ruined medieval castle of Dunluce on Northern Ireland's rugged Atlantic coastline, it's easy to imagine you are at the edge of the known universe. The castle sits on a rocky promontory surrounded by wave-lashed cliffs. It commands uninterrupted views across the Sea of Moyle. On a sunny day you can see why C.S. Lewis, author of *The Lion, the Witch and the Wardrobe*, is thought to have drawn inspiration from Dunluce when he created his magical castle of Cair Paravel, the seat of the kings and queens of the fantasy land of Narnia, its magnificent hall topped with an ivory roof and a great door looking out to the sea.

In midwinter, though, with the winds ripping across the County Antrim hills, it can be 'pretty miserable', according to Colin Breen. He should know. An archaeologist, Breen spent three years excavating an abandoned medieval town at Dunluce. 'Sometimes when we were digging there during January or February, in the middle of snow showers, you have 120 km/h gusts smashing into that space, and the roof was blown right off a farmhouse while we were working.' On days like this you can also understand why the producers of HBO's *Game of Thrones* picked Dunluce as their filming location for Castle Pyke, a fortress built on stone stacks jutting out of the sea, which, according to one character, Theon Greyjoy, is 'a hard place that breeds hard men, and hard men rule the world'. (See also 'What I Learned on My Vacation to Westeros' on page 124.)

However, Breen continues wistfully, 'you also have the complete opposite. When you're there during the summer you can see all of western Donegal in the Irish Republic, you can see the Scottish islands of Islay, Jura and Argyll. The sea is beautifully calm, and it's probably the most majestic part of this coastline. While now we have the sense of Dunluce being very much on the periphery, at the edge of this country, we forget that during the mediaeval period it was at the centre of the social world. It's during those glorious summer days, when you can see the full stretch of the north coast of Ireland, that you can appreciate Dunluce's position as the fulcrum, the pivot, of this wider world, not on the margin but very much at the centre.'

In the years the UK spent negotiating its withdrawal from the European Union, reporters from around the world headed south and west from Belfast to Northern Ireland's land frontier with the Irish Republic to assess the implications of Brexit for a peace process that brought to an end a thirty-year conflict that cost 3,500 lives. At one EU summit the Irish Taoiseach (prime minister) at the time, Leo Varadkar, brandished a newspaper cutting about a 1970s bomb attack on a border customs post as a warning to his fellow European leaders about what might happen if the Brexit negotiations failed.

MARK DEVENPORT is an English journalist and reporter. He worked for the BBC for over thirty years first as Northern Ireland correspondent, then as the network's United Nations correspondent in New York and finally as political editor at BBC Northern Ireland. In 1997, with David Sharrock, he published *Man of War, Man of Peace? The Unauthorized Biography of Gerry Adams* (Macmillan) about Irish republican politician Gerry Adams and his role in the conflict in Northern Ireland. In 2000 Devenport published an autobiographical account called *Flash Frames: Twelve Years Reporting Belfast* (Blackstaff).

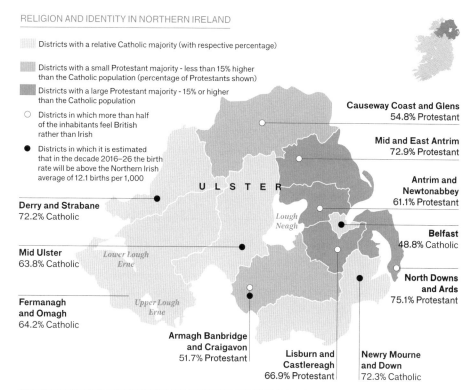

Districts with a relative Catholic majority (with respective percentage)

Districts with a small Protestant majority - less than 15% higher than the Catholic population (percentage of Protestants shown)

Districts with a large Protestant majority - 15% or higher than the Catholic population

○ Districts in which more than half of the inhabitants feel British rather than Irish

● Districts in which it is estimated that in the decade 2016–26 the birth rate will be above the Northern Irish average of 12.1 births per 1,000

Causeway Coast and Glens
54.8% Protestant

Mid and East Antrim
72.9% Protestant

Antrim and Newtonabbey
61.1% Protestant

Derry and Strabane
72.2% Catholic

U L S T E R

Lough Neagh

Belfast
48.8% Catholic

Mid Ulster
63.8% Catholic

Lower Lough Erne

North Downs and Ards
75.1% Protestant

Fermanagh and Omagh
64.2% Catholic

Upper Lough Erne

Armagh Banbridge and Craigavon
51.7% Protestant

Lisburn and Castlereagh
66.9% Protestant

Newry Mourne and Down
72.3% Catholic

SOURCE: 2011 CENSUS, NORTHERN IRELAND STATISTICS AND RESEARCH AGENCY

Everyone took Northern Ireland's sea border with Great Britain to the north and east of Belfast pretty much for granted. But then Boris Johnson, the British prime minister, cut a deal which involved keeping Northern Ireland in the EU Single Market. The arrangement meant there would be no customs checks on the land frontier. It avoided the construction of new border posts, which might in time become targets for violent extremists. It promised advantages for local manufacturers by granting Northern Ireland access to both the EU and UK markets. However, the price to be paid was a new system of checks on goods moving by ferry from Great Britain to Northern Ireland, involving a mountain of paperwork and charges that initially proved so onerous that some GB suppliers gave up doing business with their clients in Northern Ireland altogether.

If paperwork had been the only difficulty that might have been a price worth paying, but pro-British Protestant unionists sensed a threat to the links with Great Britain they have cherished ever since their forefathers migrated from Scotland

'The Protestant settlers have long enjoyed a love-hate relationship with governments in London, pledging loyalty to them while at the same time suspicious that English politicians might betray them.'

and England back in the 1600s. The Protestant settlers have long enjoyed a love-hate relationship with governments in London, pledging loyalty to them while at the same time suspicious that English politicians might betray them.

Before he became prime minister, Boris Johnson made a speech to a gathering of Northern Ireland's biggest unionist party, the Democratic Unionist Party, in which he guaranteed he would never countenance putting a border down the Irish Sea. Then the checks on the cargo arriving at the ferry ports went operational. The unionists concluded Johnson had gone back on his word. They also turned their ire on the EU, accusing it of using Northern Ireland as a plaything and deliberately pushing it into the economic clutches of the Irish government.

Disquiet over the new economic sea border was a factor in some of the worst sectarian rioting Belfast has seen in years, trouble that flared up initially in pro-British loyalist districts in April 2021. It also lay behind the removal from office of Northern Ireland's first female first minister, Arlene Foster. Representatives of pro-British loyalist paramilitary groups complained that the new trading arrangements undermined guarantees they had been given under the Good Friday Agreement peace deal of 1998. Unionist politicians involved in negotiating that deal concurred.

Irish nationalists disagreed, insisting the principles of the Good Friday Agreement remain intact and blaming the unionists for backing Brexit in the first place. Either way, the concerns over the new sea border drew the focus away from the land frontier, the scene of so much bloodshed during the Troubles of the 1970s, 1980s and 1990s. Attention shifted to the ports of Belfast, Larne and Warrenpoint where the passenger ferries and cargo ships bring in much of the food and medicine that stock Northern Ireland's supermarket and pharmacy shelves, the east–west movement of goods taken for granted for many years and which is vital in holding the United Kingdom of Great Britain and Northern Ireland together.

No one could describe Larne as an architectural gem. The County Antrim harbour town is built around the terminal from where ferries regularly set sail to Cairnryan in Scotland. Its skyline is dominated by a massive gas-fired power station at nearby Ballylumford. Larne is strongly pro-British, and graffiti appeared on its walls opposing the sea-border checks and, in some cases, threatening any staff helping to implement them. For a few days the local council withdrew employees from the sea-border checkpoints, although this move proved controversial when nationalist and centre-ground politicians questioned how

There is no precise date for the beginning of the Troubles, the conflict that brought bloodshed to Northern Ireland for thirty years, claiming the lives of roughly 3,600 people, more than half of them civilians. It grew out of a series of events between 1966 and 1969 linked to the movement for civil rights for the Catholic minority and its repression by the devolved government. In spite of the use of the terms Protestant and Catholic to refer to the two sides, the conflict was political and nationalist in nature rather than religious, revolving around the issue of the region's status: unionists and loyalists, for the most part Protestant, wanted to remain in the United Kingdom, whereas predominantly Catholic nationalists and republicans wanted a united Ireland. As well as the British Army and the local police force, the Royal Ulster Constabulary, the main participants were paramilitary organisations: the nationalist Provisional IRA – responsible for 60 per cent of the victims – and the unionist Ulster Volunteer Force and Ulster Defence Association, with 30 per cent. The conflict was characterised by guerrilla tactics, terrorism and reprisals but also internal feuds within the paramilitary groups, collusion between the army and the loyalists, assassinations, detention without trial and acts of civil disobedience – a spiral of violence that left behind traumas that have not been erased by the 1998 peace agreement (see 'The Good Friday Agreement' on page 120). Many of the murders have gone unpunished – the result of successive amnesties and offers of immunity in exchange for information – and probably never will be in the light of the ban on new criminal prosecutions announced by UK prime minister Boris Johnson in 2021 in order to 'draw a line under the Troubles'.

serious the threats really were. Within days the staff returned to their duties.

Larne might not be a tourist magnet, but it is worth the trip as it is the gateway to the gorgeous Antrim coast road. The A2 sneaks its way north from Larne up past the U-shaped glacial valleys known as the Glens of Antrim before leading on to Northern Ireland's single most popular tourist attraction, the extraordinary array of forty thousand hexagonal basalt columns jutting out into the sea known as the Giant's Causeway. Then you can continue your drive west through Bushmills – home to the distillery that makes Ireland's most famous whiskey – and on to Dunluce Castle and the beach resorts of Portstewart and Portrush, the latter of which hosts one of the world's most celebrated links golf courses.

I have lived in Northern Ireland for more than thirty years and still cherish memories of my first weekend after moving over from England when a family friend took me for a day trip up the coast. We diverted away from the shore to climb the steps beside the enchanting Glenariff waterfalls before calling in on the workshop of champion Irish fiddler and violinmaker Jim McKillop. Jim treated us to an impromptu recital of Irish reels and jigs accompanied by a plate of tomato sandwiches washed down with a tumbler of Bushmills.

That day trip might well have been one

Top: The Giant's Causeway is a natural outcrop of approximately forty thousand interlocking basalt columns of volcanic origin, the result of an ancient eruption into a fissure in the earth's crust. It is located in County Antrim, about five kilometres northeast of the town of Bushmills on the north coast of Northern Ireland.
Below: The border between County Londonderry in the United Kingdom and County Donegal in the Republic of Ireland.

'There are innumerable historic links that tie the people of the north of Ireland and their neighbours in Scotland together ... The early medieval kingdom of Dál Riata spanned both the north-east of Ireland and the islands and mainland of south-west Scotland.'

of the reasons why I decided to stay in Northern Ireland. One other impression that stuck in my English mind was the surprising proximity of Scotland, clearly visible from our car window just twenty kilometres away on the other side of the North Channel, a strait of water the late historian Jonathan Bardon described as 'the narrow sea'.

There are innumerable historic links that tie the people of the north of Ireland and their neighbours in Scotland together. In the days when Ireland was covered in forests the narrow sea wasn't a barrier but, as Bardon puts it, 'a conduit, a routeway, where peoples and cultures constantly blended'. The early medieval kingdom of Dál Riata spanned both the north-east of Ireland and the islands and mainland of south-west Scotland.

Taking the ruined castle of Dunluce as an example, archaeologist Colin Breen tells me the McQuillans, who built the place, came over to Ireland from Scotland in the 1200s as mercenaries. They were rewarded for their fighting prowess with what was known as 'sword land' in and around Dunluce and reinvented themselves as Gaelic Irish. The McQuillans dominated other local clans in near constant battles for three hundred years but made a fatal mistake around 1550 when they invited the McDonnells from the Scottish island of Islay to help them out in their latest struggle. The McDonnells promptly outmuscled the McQuillans and took over their land, including Dunluce, establishing their dominance across County Antrim.

In the 1600s the Earl of Antrim, Randal McDonnell, tried to develop a model town beside his castle, building houses for merchants trading in animal hides and cattle. Some settlers came from far afield – coins from Lithuania were among the artefacts recovered in the Dunluce excavation. The economic experiment failed, in part through the lack of an adequate local harbour, but elsewhere the plantation – the arrival of settlers from Scotland and England – gathered pace. This influx of people helps explain many of the arguments the EU and UK are still chewing over in the 21st century.

First Dunluce's town and then, hundreds of years later, its castle fell into disuse. According to one story the castle kitchen and all the McDonnells' servants with the exception of one serving boy tumbled into the sea when the rock crumbled away halfway through a lavish banquet. Breen tells me not to believe everything I read. In his professional opinion only the castle's oven was lost to the waves during the incident in the 1630s (which was great news for the kitchen staff, even if it doesn't make for quite such a good story). Now without a roof or an oven you couldn't prepare a banquet at Dunluce, but the castle's battered walls still convey a sense of its former glory.

These days, just like Dunluce Castle,

'Arguments over Northern Ireland's status within the UK have been central to the political instability that has plagued the region periodically since its separation from the rest of Ireland a century ago.'

Northern Ireland finds itself clinging to the edge. Geographically and politically it's at the periphery of two unions: the United Kingdom and the European Union. On the upside, maintaining a foothold in two major economic markets should provide canny manufacturers with an advantage. Local pharmaceutical firms, for example, will continue to have their drugs licensed for both the EU and the UK and participate in European trials. Meat and dairy farmers, vital to the Northern Ireland economy, can continue to move their products across the land frontier for processing at facilities in the Irish Republic. When the deal was done, some Scottish politicians expressed envy over Northern Ireland's special economic status. However, the downside for consumers was disruption to the normal supply of goods. North–south trade within Ireland increased initially as retailers sought to substitute products they had previously sourced from Great Britain. But simply uprooting long-established trading relationships wasn't always feasible or cost effective. Manufacturers reliant on components made in England or Scotland faced increased cost and delay.

Beyond the pure economics, though, the trade checks ushered in by the new EU–UK protocol stirred wider political and cultural anxieties. Irish-nationalist and centre-ground politicians and their supporters felt any 'teething problems' with the new rules would ultimately prove worth while if they ensured the free flow of goods and people across the frontier with the Irish Republic, but many unionists expressed outrage that the London government could contemplate requiring firms from other parts of the UK to fill in forms and submit to checks if they wanted to do business with their fellow British citizens. For these unionists the protocol amounted to a fundamental erosion of their identity, an 'economic annexation', pushing Northern Ireland ever further to the periphery of the UK by making its people semi-detached citizens of their own country.

A Westminster parliamentary committee that scrutinises policy regarding Northern Ireland took evidence from a series of concerned pro-British loyalists, with the chair, English Conservative Member of Parliament Simon Hoare, repeatedly trying to reassure his witnesses that the new rules applied to goods not people so could not amount to an erosion of their national identity. Over social media Hoare argued that if firms in his English county of Dorset were 'offered a foot in the UK Internal Market and the EU Single Market most would bite your hand off'. However, a unionist retorted that 'the people of Dorset would [not] appreciate a border between them and [the neighbouring English counties of] Devon, Somerset and Wiltshire'. Hoare's committee heard a teenage loyalist activist, Joel Keys, declare that while he

THE PASSENGER   Mark Devenport

was 'no fan of violence' he 'would not rule it off the table' if the campaign against the trade checks continued into the future without success. The Conservative MP declared this piece of evidence to his committee to be 'incredibly worrying and dispiriting'.

Arguments over Northern Ireland's status within the UK have been central to the political instability that has plagued the region periodically since its separation from the rest of Ireland a century ago, but the role of the European Union in the region tended to be much more low key during the forty-three years following both the UK and the Republic of Ireland joining the old EEC club in 1973. Financial support from Brussels massively improved the Irish Republic's previously ramshackle roads and infrastructure, laying the groundwork for a period of rapid economic growth in the 1990s and early 2000s nicknamed the 'Celtic Tiger' years. In Northern Ireland during the 1970s, 1980s and early 1990s – the years the Troubles raged – unemployment was high and the economy heavily dependent on massive financial subsidies from London. But the birth of the European Single Market in 1993 cleared away remaining obstacles to trade between the north and south of Ireland. Coincidentally the paramilitary ceasefires of 1994 opened up new opportunities for political progress.

The EU pumped more than €3 billion ($3.5 billion) into Northern Ireland and the Irish counties just south of the land frontier in an effort to shore up economic development and reconciliation. While American politicians such as the former president, Bill Clinton, tended to get the kudos and media attention for their efforts in giving the delicate negotiations a helping hand, the rusty wheels

THE SAUSAGE WAR

During the difficult post-Brexit negotiations between the European Union and the UK the only thing that the two sides agreed upon was to protect the 1998 peace agreement at all costs (see 'The Good Friday Agreement' on page 120), which entailed keeping the land border between Northern Ireland and the Republic of Ireland open without reintroducing infrastructure such as cameras and border posts, which were magnets for republican attacks during the Troubles. So it was agreed that Northern Ireland would retain membership of the European Single Market, ensuring the free passage of goods and people across the border. Customs and phytosanitary checks required by the EU for products entering from Great Britain (as a non-EU country) would take place at Northern Irish ports instead. The Brexit agreement, which came into force in January 2021, contained a moratorium to give the UK enough time to put systems in place to check goods arriving in Belfast, but six months later, when the moratorium expired, the systems were not yet operating amid an atmosphere of distrust and reciprocal accusations and threats. As always, the consequences were felt by the people of Northern Ireland: delays, bureaucratic issues and supermarket shortages, particularly of chilled meat products, which were banned under EU food safety standards. The 'sausage war', as it was dubbed by the British press, reinforced the widely held belief among loyalists in Northern Ireland that their country was being used as a battleground for disputes between the EU and the UK that actually had little or nothing to do with Northern Ireland.

of the political process were undoubtedly oiled by the EU's special Peace Fund and its cross-border Interreg project-funding programme. EU money helped fund developments like the Peace Bridge spanning the River Foyle in Derry/Londonderry (even the name of Northern Ireland's second city is a source of contention between nationalists and unionists) and the transformation of what had been a frequently attacked military barracks in north Belfast into a cross-community sports centre.

The EU's largesse was generally well received, although they got a taste of the intractable nature of the divide in Northern Ireland when they pledged millions of euros to an ambitious plan to transform the region's most notorious jail – where Irish Republican Army (IRA) prisoners once starved themselves to death on hunger strike – into an EU-branded Peace and Conflict Transformation Centre. EU signage was erected on the site of the former Maze jail, and an internationally renowned architect drew up plans for the new centre, only for the project to be scrapped in 2013 after pro-British unionists expressed their fears that it would end up being a 'shrine' to the IRA prisoners who lost their lives there.

The Maze controversy served as a reminder to EU bureaucrats of the continuing sensitivies of post-Troubles Northern Ireland, but they were not the target of either side's ire, still occupying the role of neutral benefactors. However, all that changed three years later with the Brexit referendum. Most (but by no means all) unionists sided with Boris Johnson in advocating withdrawal from the EU. Irish nationalists, centre-ground politicians and some unionists wanted to remain (with two former British prime ministers who had played key roles in the peace process, John Major and Tony Blair, both warning of the potential for disruption to trade and wider relations in Ireland if the UK did not stay in the EU). In the end, 56 per cent of voters in Northern Ireland backed Remain, but the UK as a whole voted narrowly to leave. Since then prime ministers Theresa May and Boris Johnson have wrestled with the consequences of the referendum. Even though the EU has continued its funding efforts (through a Peace Plus programme) and afforded Northern Irish students continuing access to programmes such as the Erasmus university-exchange scheme, pro-British unionists have increasingly stopped seeing the EU as an impartial well-wisher and viewed it more as a partisan political player, happy to side with Irish nationalists in the old argument about Northern Ireland's British or Irish identity.

Northern Ireland was created a century ago as a redoubt for the pro-British Protestant settlers in Ireland, while the rest of the island rose up against British rule in a struggle for independence. The way the land frontier was drawn – carving out six of Ireland's thirty-two counties – deliberately ensured the Protestants enjoyed a two-to-one majority over their Catholic neighbours. That majority remained intact for decades but has now been eroded to the extent that the two communities are almost equal in number.

As a very rough rule of thumb, the closer to the land frontier you get the more likely you are to be in Catholic Irish-nationalist territory, while the nearer you are to the narrow sea the greater the chance you will find yourself among Protestant pro-British unionists, so it was no coincidence that North Antrim – the parliamentary constituency which includes the Giant's Causeway and much

At the beginning of the 20th century the whole of Ireland is part of the United Kingdom of Great Britain and Ireland. Unlike the rest of the UK it has a majority Catholic population, except in Ulster, the wealthiest province, which is home to descendants of English and Scottish Protestant settlers. For decades republican Irish nationalists, represented politically by Sinn Féin after the party's foundation in 1905, have waged a campaign for Home Rule and self-government but face fierce opposition from Ulster unionists, who threaten to use force and propose that the province should not be included in any Home Rule or independence agreements.

1916

On Easter Monday an uprising breaks out in Dublin but is quickly put down by the army. The brutal execution of a number of rebels achieves what the revolt was unable to inspire: a change in public opinion in favour of republicanism and independence.

1919

Following its electoral successes in 1918 Sinn Féin boycotts the Westminster Parliament, establishing an Irish assembly and declaring independence. Elements of the Irish Republican Army (IRA) launch the War of Independence. The republicans, led by Michael Collins, adopt guerrilla tactics. In Ulster the conflict takes on sectarian overtones, with massacres of Catholics carried out by the Protestant police in reprisal for the IRA's actions.

1921

The British Parliament passes the Government of Ireland Act separating six of the nine counties of Ulster from the rest of Ireland to create Northern Ireland with the border intended to ensure an internal Protestant majority. This partition effectively clears the way for negotiations that lead to the creation of the Irish Free State in 1922, after a brief but violent civil war between supporters of the treaty (including Michael Collins, who is killed in the conflict) and its opponents (including the future prime minister and president Éamon de Valera), who are defeated.

1924

The Boundary Commission (with commissioners from Britain, the Irish Free State and Northern Ireland) meets for the first time to discuss the border between the two parts of the island, proposing a territorial exchange, but is ignored. As a result, the Ulster Unionist Party is guaranteed fifty years of uninterrupted rule and puts in place policies that discriminate against the Catholic minority.

1937

A new constitution put forward by Éamon de Valera replaces the Irish Free State with the Republic of Ireland, Éire in Gaelic. The constitution also declares the intention of the Irish people to reunify the island by peaceful means. A year earlier de Valera had banned the IRA, which in the meantime had become a far-left-leaning organisation.

1941

In the Belfast blitz, the Luftwaffe bombs the Northern Irish capital several times, destroying the port and the shipyards, killing hundreds of people and damaging fifty thousand houses. Éire remains officially neutral, although works secretly with the Allies.

1949

Éire leaves the Commonwealth of Nations and becomes a fully fledged independent republic. In 1955 it joins the UN.

1966–9

Civil rights marches held by the Catholic population cause tensions with and violent reactions from unionists. Paramilitary groups are established, and after the communal riot known as the Battle of the Bogside, in a Catholic area of Derry/Londonderry, the British state intervenes, deploying the army. This signals the start of the Troubles.

1972

On Bloody Sunday, 30 January, the British Army's Parachute Regiment opens fire on a crowd of demonstrators in Derry/Londonderry, killing fourteen. The episode swells the ranks of the Provisional IRA, whose recruitment is also helped by the British government's policy of internment without trial. This is the bloodiest year of the conflict, with 472 people losing their lives.

1973

The United Kingdom and the Republic of Ireland join the European Economic Community. The IRA carries out its first bombings in England.

1976

London abolishes political-prisoner status for paramilitary detainees. The IRA, after a change of leadership, responds with a campaign of killings targeting prison officers. The so-called 'blanket protest' begins at Long Kesh Detention Centre, later renamed the Maze Prison. Prisoners refuse to wear prison uniform, dressing in nothing but a blanket. This is followed by the dirty protest, in which they smear their own excrement on their cell walls.

1981

Bobby Sands, commanding officer of the IRA prisoners in Long Kesh, dies after sixty-six days of hunger strike. Another ten prisoners die of starvation before the strike is called off. The strike fails in its immediate aims, but within the republican movement Sinn Féin starts to become increasingly important.

1988

The founder of the republican Northern Irish Social Democratic and Labour Party, John Hume, meets Gerry Adams of Sinn Féin.

1998

After a new ceasefire in 1997 the representatives of Northern Ireland's political parties sign the Belfast Agreement, also known as the Good Friday Agreement, which establishes self-government for Northern Ireland and the future possibility of a united Ireland to be decided by referendum. The Real IRA, formed by dissidents opposed to the peace process, detonates a car bomb in Omagh, killing twenty-nine people in what was the deadliest single attack of the conflict.

2005

The IRA announces the end of its armed struggle. Attacks staged by dissident groups like the Real IRA (later the New IRA) and the Continuity IRA continue.

2016

The United Kingdom as a whole votes to leave the European Union. The referendum result in Northern Ireland is 56 per cent in favour of Remain. Fears over the reintroduction of a border between Northern Ireland and the Republic of Ireland reignite tensions between unionists and nationalists, and the issue becomes one of the crucial points in the post-Brexit talks between the EU and the UK.

1993

Customs posts between Northern Ireland and the Republic of Ireland, which had been the target of numerous attacks during the Troubles, are removed when the European Single Market comes into force. The IRA – now armed by Colonel Gaddafi of Libya – sets off two huge bombs in the City of London in 1992 and 1993.

2020

The EU and the UK agree to the so-called Northern Ireland Protocol, which introduces a customs border for goods in the Irish Sea, provoking the anger of unionists who see Northern Ireland's separation from Great Britain regarding trade as a prelude to the unification of Ireland.

1994

After secret talks between the British government and the republican movement the IRA and Protestant paramilitary groups announce a ceasefire. The exclusion of Sinn Féin from the peace talks leads to the end of the truce two years later.

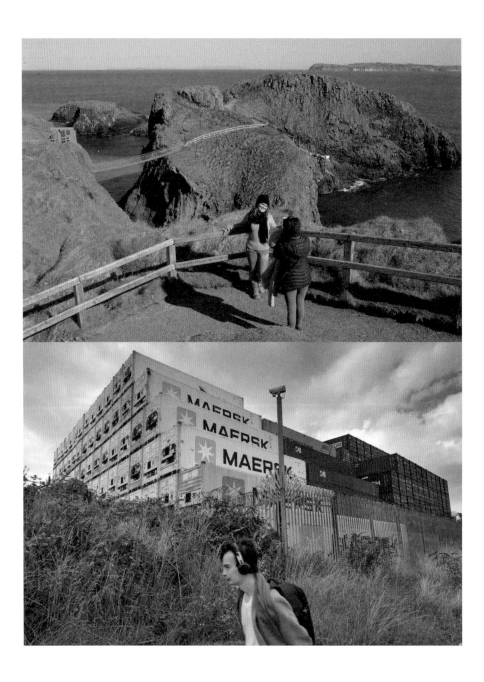

Top: Carrick-a-Rede Rope Bridge in Ballintoy, County Antrim.
Below: Shipping containers in Dublin Port.

'The closer to the land frontier you get the more likely you are to be in Catholic Irish-nationalist territory, while the nearer you are to the narrow sea the greater the chance you will find yourself among Protestant pro-British unionists.'

of the spectacular coast road – was for forty years represented by that most militant of unionists, the evangelical Protestant preacher the Reverend Ian Paisley.

For most of his long career Paisley was known as the 'Dr No' of Northern Ireland politics, a protest politician who would reject any hint of compromise, quick to denounce his Irish-nationalist opponents and the Catholic Church that they revered. Initially Paisley regarded the European Union as a conspiracy to create a Catholic superstate, and in 1988, as a Member of the European Parliament, he interrupted a speech to the European Parliament by Pope John Paul II shouting, 'I denounce you as the Antichrist!' In later years, though, Paisley mellowed, joining with nationalists like the Nobel Peace Prize-winner John Hume in ensuring Northern Ireland benefited from European grants. Then, astonishingly, he reached a deal to share power with his erstwhile Irish-republican enemies. In 2007 his conversion both to power sharing and working with the European Union seemed complete when I covered a news conference during which the octogenarian Paisley laughed and joked with the senior EU diplomat José Manuel Barroso. All antipathy towards Brussels seemed forgotten as Paisley told Barroso Northern Ireland produced the finest food in all Europe and extolled the virtues of 'fadge' potato bread, a local

delicacy the Portuguese diplomat could be forgiven for never having previously tasted.

Ian Paisley died in 2014, but these days North Antrim is represented by his son and namesake, Ian Paisley Jr. Ian Jr inherited his father's scepticism regarding the EU, strongly supporting Brexit in the 2016 referendum. Now, in common with other unionists, he rails against the sea border as a betrayal of the UK-wide Brexit he had hoped to achieve. Ian Jr emphasises that his enthusiasm for Brexit shouldn't be mistaken for any antipathy towards individual Europeans, whom he hopes will continue to come and visit the 'majestic rugged beauty' of his North Antrim constituency. He tells me Brexit is about 'trade relationships, not personal relationships. I'm not less European because I don't want to be part of the EU. Are the Swiss less European because they have never been part of it? I don't think so. We are an island. We have an island mentality, and wanting to do it our own way is something that's not unusual for island folk. It was about opposition to the bureaucracy of the European community, it was not about opposition to Europeans.'

During the post-Brexit negotiations Paisley Jr didn't think either Brussels or London paid enough attention to how important trade and relationships across the narrow sea were for people in Northern Ireland. 'They probably didn't recognise that actually it's a mainstay of daily life, and whether it's someone wanting to nip over to Scotland for the weekend with their dog or someone wanting to trade their cattle back and forth or bigger business relationships, all of those things have been disrupted. I don't think anyone understands how close that relationship is, and to interfere with it in such a dynamic way as the [EU–UK] protocol has done, it really has caused severe disruption.'

Paisley Jr is optimistic that a long-term resolution can be found. Despite his support for Brexit, he acknowledges that, during Northern Ireland's peace process, EU funding played a constructive role. He urges the EU to remain even handed in its dealings with Northern Ireland in the future, arguing that 'it's important anyone from the outside comes with a very open mind and appreciates there are two sides here, and there's not one side that is entirely right and not one side that's entirely wrong'.

While Protestants and unionists might be in a majority in North Antrim, that doesn't mean there isn't a significant Catholic Irish-nationalist community there. The picturesque Antrim coast village of Cushendall is where Alasdair McDonnell grew up. Now in his seventies, McDonnell appreciates the natural splendour of the Antrim Glens. But, when he was looking after cattle and sheep on his family farm as an eight-year-old boy back in the 1950s, he had other things on his mind. In the winter, he tells me, 'I could find myself on top of a mountain trying to herd sheep in a storm, running the risk of getting blown over a cliff by the wind. It tempers your appreciation of the beauty of the countryside. Survival was the name of the game.' That said, the Glens exert 'a tremendous emotional pull later in life', and McDonnell 'never fails to get a glow inside' as he drives up the coast road towards his childhood home.

The boy who looked after sheep went on to qualify as a doctor then became a politician. In 2011 he was elected leader of the Social Democratic and Labour Party, an Irish-nationalist party founded by the late John Hume. Many regard Hume as the principal architect of the Irish peace process. Famously, Hume credited the European Union as 'the best example in the history of the world of conflict resolution' and recalled his first walk across the bridge near the European Parliament in Strasbourg, which links France and Germany, as a moment of inspiration for his work building bridges back in Ireland.

Like John Hume, Alasdair McDonnell describes himself as 'a passionate European' who believes 'the European Union is a very solid bulwark against the sort of savagery we saw in the world wars. That, for me, is the priority – it's peace and stability and creating a space where the nations of Europe can engage positively and constructively.' McDonnell 'became very anxious when the UK decided to hold a Brexit referendum because I saw the potential for the whole thing going wrong. I believed stability was everything. I believe society and the government needs to move forward incrementally rather than having shockwaves like Brexit.'

While unionist politicians angrily denounce the EU's handling of Northern Ireland in the wake of Brexit, McDonnell thinks 'Europe has been very tolerant of the madness, and I see Brexit as a madness on the part of a section of the British political community, which has done Britain serious damage'. He blames 'a very well-organised minority within the British Conservative Party which is driving a Little England agenda'. Although

> 'While Protestants remain in the majority in North Antrim, a census taken in 2021 is expected to show that across Northern Ireland neither the Protestant nor the Catholic communities will exceed 50 per cent.'

his party aspires towards a united Ireland, McDonnell takes no satisfaction in what he regards as the 'shambolic instability' demonstrated by the UK government. The proximity to Scotland of his home village convinces him of the need to maintain strong and stable relationships between Ireland and Great Britain.

McDonnell understands unionist complaints about the disruption the new economic sea border causes to aspects of daily life. Because he grew up on the Antrim coast he's steeped in the connections across the narrow sea, recalling the days before budget flights when Glaswegians would head across to Northern Ireland for their summer breaks. 'A lot of the tourist trade when I was a child was Scottish, a lot of people went to work in Glasgow, and many of them came back and rented houses where I lived.' McDonnell grew up hearing tales of the early 20th century when the Auld Lammas Fair – an annual get-together in the harbour town of Ballycastle – used to attract large contingents from the Scottish Isles keen to sample, among other things, dulse and yellow man, an unlikely combination of honeycomb toffee and purple seaweed traditionally served up at the fair.

Despite his background, McDonnell doesn't agree with unionist demands that the new Irish Sea trade checks be scrapped. Once Brexit happened, McDonnell insists, 'it was unavoidable,

there had to be a boundary somewhere', and Northern Ireland's seaports were 'the most appropriate place' for any checks. He wants those checks to 'be as efficient and as effective as possible, as simple and as unobstructive as possible', adding that in his view the protocol that governs Northern Ireland's trade does not impact on its 'jurisdiction or sovereignty but the social and commercial aspects. The protocol is the price we pay for Brexit.'

While Protestants remain in the majority in North Antrim, a census taken in 2021 is expected to show that across Northern Ireland neither the Protestant nor the Catholic communities will exceed 50 per cent. The balance is expected to be held by those who don't identify with either camp. These figures aren't just of academic interest. When they are published in 2022 the details will be studied closely by political parties and the British and Irish governments looking for any clues they might provide about the likely result of a future referendum on Irish unity. The 'others' who don't fit neatly into the traditional unionist or nationalist camps could hold the key to the future in their hands.

As the daughter of a north-coast Presbyterian father and a Dublin Catholic mother, Alison Grundle has a foot in both camps. Grundle is a business consultant who lives about five kilometres away from Dunluce Castle. It's a place she feels a special affinity with, dating back to the days when her father used to joke that the castle was rightfully their home. The family connection is via Alison's paternal grandmother, who traced her roots back to the McQuillans, the clan who built Dunluce around the year 1500. As a child Alison remembers her parents receiving a grant from a local authority to improve their house, and she took the family story so seriously she asked her father if he could apply for another grant to put a roof on the ruined castle so they could move back and live there again.

Grundle has worked as an adviser for a unionist justice minister in Northern Ireland's local government, but she doesn't identify herself as a unionist. She shared John Hume's hope that membership of the EU 'might bring a solution to the conflict on this island, that we could move to a position whereby nationalism in both its forms, British nationalism and Irish nationalism, would recede and the cultural differences between us could be something that we celebrate rather than a source of friction and discontent. That did not happen.'

In 2016, when the UK held its Brexit referendum, Grundle voted to remain in the EU 'because I believe no British Conservative government would provide Northern Ireland with the funding that we got from Europe and because I thought Brexit would cause discontent. The border has to go somewhere. What we have with the protocol and the sea border is a very unsatisfactory situation, but it was always going to be unsatisfactory.'

Grundle worries that the current trade arrangements have left Northern Ireland 'in the worst of all possible worlds', with the rest of the UK 'getting on with its post-Brexit future while we have to live with it in perpetuity, with our politicians voting on the sea-border checks every four years. That means Brexit will be ever present, and the sovereignty issue, through Brexit, has gained a whole new lease of life. So in that respect Brexit has been a disaster for any chance of furthering the peace process here.'

Looking to the future, Grundle urges the EU to 'understand the fears that exist within unionism. There is a genuine element to it, and dismissing those fears doesn't help anyone. The EU needs to make the trade protocol work. A risk-based approach [assessing the genuine risk of UK goods making their way illegally into the EU Single Market] rather than a rigid rules-based approach will help a lot with that.'

Fearing that the instability triggered by Brexit and the trade protocol could hamstring the local economy, Alison Grundle believes both the UK and EU must finance a major investment fund to help Northern Ireland face the challenges ahead. Certainly the picturesque north-east coast provides plenty of evidence of the potential for Northern Ireland's economy to prosper in the future. Here tourism will always be a major driver. The unique volcanic rock formations at the Giant's Causeway have been attracting visitors to the area for centuries. Before the pandemic struck, the Causeway was bringing in an estimated one million tourists per year, with perhaps fifty coaches a day arriving at the peak of the season. Then there are other attractions, such as Dunluce (which, by comparison with the Causeway, has very constrained parking and visitor facilities), the dramatic rope bridge at Carrick-a-Rede, the Dark Hedges made famous by their appearance in *Game of Thrones* and – near the ferry terminal of Larne – the Gobbins Cliff Path.

Top: Signs in the town of Larne, Northern Ireland, protesting against the border in the Irish Sea brought in as part of the Northern Ireland Protocol agreed between the UK and the EU.
Below: The port of Larne.

Data in %, 2020

A Which of these definitions best describes you?

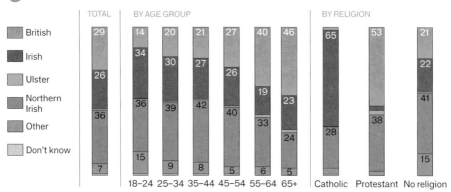

British — Irish — Ulster — Northern Irish — Other — Don't know

TOTAL | BY AGE GROUP | BY RELIGION

18–24 25–34 35–44 45–54 55–64 65+ | Catholic Protestant No religion

B Do you think the UK's exit from the EU has made the possibility of a united Ireland more likely, less likely or no difference?

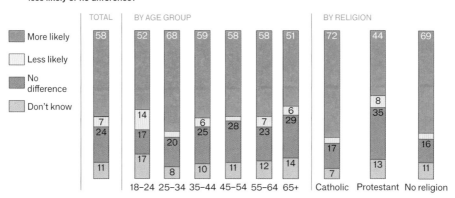

More likely — Less likely — No difference — Don't know

TOTAL | BY AGE GROUP | BY RELIGION

18–24 25–34 35–44 45–54 55–64 65+ | Catholic Protestant No religion

C If there was a referendum on the future of Northern Ireland tomorrow, would you vote yes or no to unification with the Republic of Ireland?

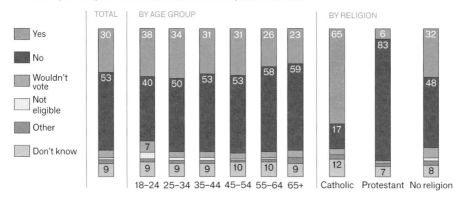

Yes — No — Wouldn't vote — Not eligible — Other — Don't know

TOTAL | BY AGE GROUP | BY RELIGION

18–24 25–34 35–44 45–54 55–64 65+ | Catholic Protestant No religion

SOURCE: 2020 NORTHERN IRELAND LIFE AND TIMES SURVEY

> 'According to Irish mythology the Giant's Causeway was a bridge over which Scottish and Irish giants could make their way if they wanted a battle.'

The Gobbins markets itself as Europe's most dramatic coastal walk. The path includes a series of bridges and tunnels, which make their way around the cliffs of Islandmagee. It was originally constructed in 1902, at the instigation of a visionary Irish engineer called Berkeley Deane Wise. The path proved an immediate draw when it opened, with one early visitor, W.J. Fennell, writing in 1902 that 'there is, in short, nothing like the Gobbins anywhere else in the world'. However, given the pounding they took from the sea, the bridges and platforms carrying the path required constant maintenance. Eventually landslides made the path too dangerous, and it had to be closed to visitors in the 1950s. But the Gobbins reopened in 2017 after a major renovation project saw the construction of fifteen new bridges and six galleries hugging the cliffs. Walkers are rewarded with stunning views across the narrow sea stretching as far as the volcanic Scottish island of Ailsa Craig. The walkway cost £7.5 million ($10.5 million), half of which was provided by the EU.

If both the initial construction and renovation of the Gobbins were incredible engineering feats, they are dwarfed into insignificance by another proposed construction project that has gained traction in recent times, one that would undoubtedly be a game changer as far as the Northern Ireland coast and its economy is concerned. But there's considerable scepticism over whether the project is in the realms of reality or nothing but a deliberate political distraction. According to Irish mythology the Giant's Causeway was a bridge over which Scottish and Irish giants could make their way if they wanted a battle. Now, in the febrile atmosphere engendered by the controversy over the economic sea border, there is renewed talk of the UK building a real bridge or tunnel to join its disparate regions together.

In March 2021 Boris Johnson backed a feasibility study examining the expense and practical challenges involved in constructing a fixed link between Great Britain and Northern Ireland. London newspapers published graphics showing an amalgam of bridges and tunnels crossing the Irish Sea. One showed an underground roundabout encircling the Isle of Man, a project swiftly nicknamed the 'Boris Burrow' after a leader famously keen on ambitious capital projects. Enthusiasts point to the immense bridges of China, such as the fifty-kilometre Hong Kong–Zhuhai–Macau bridge, as proof the proposed Irish Sea link isn't, like the Giant's Causeway, the stuff of myth and legend. Detractors respond by noting the extreme depth of the North Channel, the sea that separates Scotland and Northern Ireland, the fact that it is stuffed full of unstable munitions dumped after the First World War and an estimated price tag in the region of £30 billion ($40 billion).

When I interviewed Boris Johnson in the spring of 2021 he sounded a little tentative in his support for the project, acknowledging such a massive

'Long before any of us had ever heard of Brexit, Northern Ireland's new economic sea border or Ireland's hundred-year-old land frontier, different quarrels raged across these islands and this rugged coastline.'

undertaking wouldn't be 'easy or an absolute slam dunk', but he urged me to 'look at what they've been doing in Norway, look at what the Chinese have done. Why don't we at least look at this idea?'

The proposal for a bridge across the Irish Sea has, in fact, been around for more than 150 years, and back in the 1950s a Northern Irish MP called Montgomery Hyde argued for the construction of a tunnel under the sea bed but was unable to convince the government of its practicality. Hyde maintained this was not a 'crazy idea' but didn't assist his own argument by running through a series of previous outlandish schemes, including one which envisaged using seawater to pressurise a train forward through a tunnel. Hyde admitted the proposal didn't take into account 'what would happen if the water came in at both ends'. Prime Minister Johnson pointed out to me that the tunnel between England and France 'was talked about for two centuries before it actually happened, so it may be that we are ahead of our time, but there's no time like the present'.

While the precise arguments around the feasibility of a fixed link between Scotland and Northern Ireland might be matters for engineers and financiers, the timing of the latest surge of interest in the idea cannot be separated from the fraught political aftermath of Brexit. Boris Johnson's critics regard his interest

in the project as a tactic, employed to distract attention from his broken promises over the sea-border checks and the growing fears of Northern Ireland's unionists that they are being shunted ever further towards the edge of the UK.

Although it's the EU trade checks that have been making the biggest headlines and provoking interventions from the likes of President Joe Biden (who has urged all sides to respect the Good Friday Agreement), there are other sources of instability on the wider UK scene that Johnson might hope to assuage with his talk of ambitious bridges and tunnels. In May 2021 Nicola Sturgeon's Scottish Nationalist Party won their fourth consecutive term in power in the devolved government in Edinburgh. Sturgeon made it clear she would seek another referendum on Scottish independence (a previous vote in 2014 was lost by 45 per cent to 55 per cent). An opinion poll commissioned by the BBC indicated most people in Northern Ireland believe any vote in favour of Scottish independence would make a united Ireland more likely. With Irish republicans agitating for a border poll to decide whether Northern Ireland should leave the UK, the same poll suggested a majority in Northern Ireland don't think the region will still be part of the UK in twenty-five years' time. Although unionists might dismiss those concerns, they have contributed to a widespread sense that, as it enters its second century, Northern Ireland is in a state of flux.

With relationships across the narrow sea badly in need of both psychological and, potentially, physical buttressing, the North Antrim MP Ian Paisley Jr tells me he thinks the idea for an Irish Sea bridge 'should definitely be explored. It certainly would allow for greater commerce, greater holiday opportunities. People pooh-poohed the original idea for the Channel Tunnel between France and England. Now they can hardly think of life without it. I think we should at least explore the option, and if the resources are there, let's do it.'

Former Irish-nationalist politician Alasdair McDonnell is 'all in favour of restoring the historic links between Northern Ireland and Scotland' but remains wary of the 'major difficulties and dangers' that would confront any engineers. He wonders whether the most sensible first step would be fixing what he regards as the unacceptable road network currently servicing Scotland's ferry terminals.

Alison Grundle says that 'if it wasn't for the depth of the sea and all the munitions dumped on the sea bed, a bridge or a tunnel wouldn't be a bad idea, you get them all over Scandinavia', but given the challenges any engineers would inevitably face in the North Channel, Grundle reckons 'for here, it's a bonkers suggestion'.

Despite their very different politics, Paisley, McDonnell and Grundle share a missionary zeal in proclaiming the wonders of the Causeway Coast, from the beautiful walks and views to the burgeoning local gastro-food scene. But Grundle has a bone to pick with McDonnell, who proudly traces his roots

back to the Earls of Antrim, the leaders of the clan who evicted Grundle's ancestors from Dunluce Castle five hundred years ago, sparking a lengthy feud. When I tell her I am talking to a McDonnell, Grundle asks me if I can extract an apology from him for stealing her family home. Alasdair McDonnell responds that this shouldn't be a problem, provided Alison can first arrange for her McQuillan clan to say sorry to Richard Óg de Burgh, a knight who built a manor on the Dunluce site before the McQuillan mercenaries arrived.

It's a reminder that long before any of us had ever heard of Brexit, Northern Ireland's new economic sea border or Ireland's hundred-year-old land frontier, different quarrels raged across these islands and along this rugged coastline. As Dunluce's ruins are now a monument in the care of the Northern Ireland Department for Communities, it's a safe bet that whoever eventually says sorry to whom, neither Alasdair nor Alison are going to be getting a grant to mend the roof or moving their possessions back into the castle any time soon. 🐦

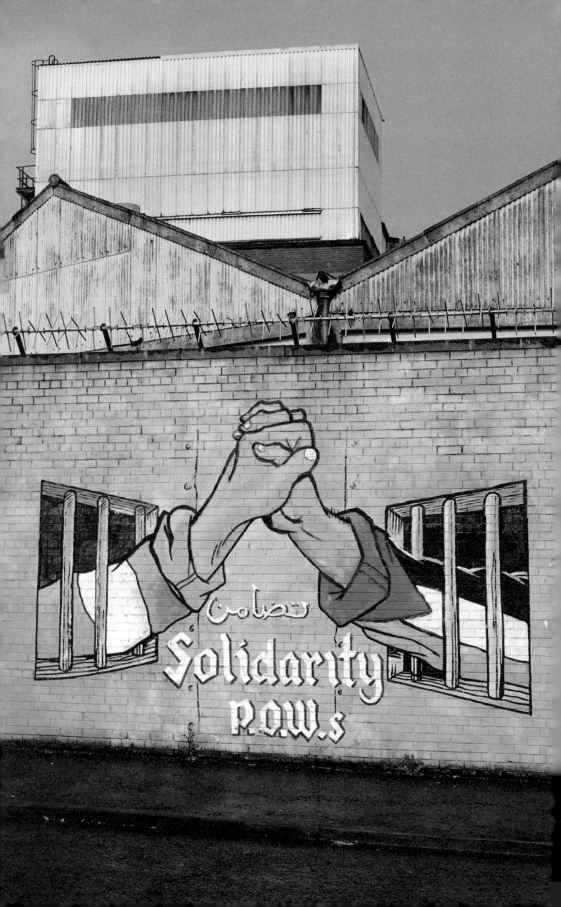

Suicide of the Ceasefire Babies

Since the signing of the Good Friday Agreement in 1998 more people in Northern Ireland have committed suicide than were killed during the thirty-year conflict. Before her murder in 2019 journalist Lyra McKee investigated this troubling phenomenon.

LYRA MCKEE

Murals advocating solidarity between Irish-nationalist and Palestinian prisoners near the Falls Road in west Belfast. The Falls Road has been synonymous with the city's Catholic community for at least a century and a half.

So the answer to your question is yes.
If you're ever really gonna kill yourself, yes, please,
Call me.

From 'I Won't Write Your Obituary' by Nora Cooper

'He's only seventeen, how can he be dead?'

For once, Big Gay Mick wasn't saying much. 'I don't know. We've just seen his stepdad getting out of a taxi at the top of the street, and he told us.'

There was no getting any other details out of him; he was in shock. Big Gay Mick was not normally lost for words. Stick-thin, with a baseball cap permanently pulled down over his eyes and a gold chain around his neck, you might have mistaken him for one of the neighbour-hood hard men until you heard his voice: shrill, camp and a fair bit higher than it should have been post-puberty. In our little teenage gang he was the only one brave enough to be openly gay. It wasn't easy.

We grew up just off Murder Mile, a stretch of the Antrim Road in Belfast, so called because of the number of casualties there during the Troubles (the wider area was known as the Murder Triangle for the same reason). On the street where Big Gay Mick lived, beside a 'peace wall' that sepa-rated us from the Protestants, loyalist paramilitaries would drive down, single out a target and pull the trigger. Even though Mick lived just two streets away from me, I wasn't allowed to go to his

until I was ten years old, two years after the Good Friday Agreement – a key part of the peace process – was signed. In an area where murder and mayhem created hard-ened men, it was not easy to be as camp as Christmas. He managed, though, all the while smirking at a member of the local paramilitary who would shout homo-phobic abuse at us as we walked by.

The swagger was gone today. I was grilling him, and he didn't have the answers I wanted.

'How can he be dead?'

'He killed himself. Apparently he escaped from the hospital. They found him in the grounds.'

I don't remember much of what happened after that, other than walking upstairs, kicking something in the bath-room and cursing Jonny for dying.

The Ceasefire Babies was what they called us. Those too young to remember the worst of the terror because we were either in nappies or just out of them when the Provisional IRA ceasefire was called. I was four, Jonny was three. We were the Good Friday Agreement generation, destined never to witness the horrors of war but to reap the spoils of peace. The spoils just never seemed to reach us.

The first time Jonny tried to kill himself the ambulance was parked just beyond

Murals commemorating key events during the
Troubles in the Bogside, a republican neighbourhood
in west Derry/Londonderry, the scene of serious
clashes in the early days of the conflict.

Lyra McKee

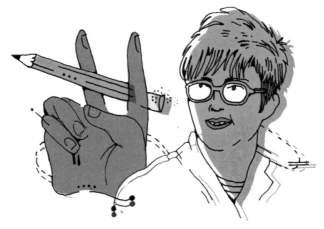

'With the signing of the Good Friday Agreement, my generation – the children and the grandchildren of the civil rights protesters – were told we would be the first to enjoy peace in decades. Just because we're not at war any more doesn't mean the shadow of the gunman has left the room,' wrote Lyra McKee in 2015. Four years later, on 18 April 2019, the 29-year-old journalist from Belfast was killed with a bullet to the head in Derry/Londonderry during clashes between dissident nationalist groups and the police. The New IRA admitted responsibility and formally apologised to the journalist's family and partner, saying that Lyra was 'tragically killed while standing beside enemy forces'. In September 2021 two men were charged with her murder. Her funeral was attended by representatives of all the political parties of Northern Ireland as well as the Irish and British governments, and the international media was filled with personal and professional tributes to Lyra. She was the rising star of Northern Irish journalism and built her career – during a period of crisis for the newspapers – on crowdsourcing, which she used to finance her investigative pieces. At the age of just sixteen – after overcoming problems caused by eyesight issues that meant she had to wear an eyepatch as a child and then very thick glasses – she won the Sky Young Journalist of the Year Award. When she was twenty-six *Forbes* included her in its '30 under 30' list of influential figures in the European media. Her reports on unsolved murders during the Troubles and the consequences of the conflict were published by *Mosaic*, the *Belfast Telegraph*, *Private Eye* and *Buzzfeed News*, and at the time of her death she was writing a book to be published by Faber and Faber. She was also an activist for LGBTQ+ rights. In what was perhaps her best-known article, 'Letter to My 14-Year-Old Self' (available on the *Guardian* website), later adapted for the screen, the then 24-year-old described the persecution she suffered at school after confiding in the 'wrong person' that she was gay. A crowdfunding campaign (www.gofundme.com/f/in-memory-of-lyra-mckee) organised to help Lyra's family has to date raised nearly £70,000 ($95,500), some of which will be used to provide bursaries to young journalists. One of the pieces of advice that Lyra gave herself in her letter was, 'It won't always be like this. It's going to get better.'

his front door, as if the paramedics were mindful of drawing attention to the house. Despite the fact that the local papers brought news of suicides every week – for some reason the numbers had rocketed – there was still an element of Catholic shame about it all. When they carted him off to hospital to pump the tablets out of his stomach his mother didn't go with him.

That night he was released. We'd formed a 'suicide watch' in preparation. 'You go in for your dinner and I'll stay with him, and then I'll go in for my dinner when you come back.' When he joined us little was said. We didn't ask him why he'd done it. He was only sixteen, the rest of us a year or two older. To our teenage brains suicide was like cancer, an accident of fate. Sometimes people survived it, and sometimes they didn't. The newspapers, bringing reports of more deaths every week, spoke of it like a disease, using words like 'epidemic'. It never occurred to us, as we took turns to keep an eye on Jonny that night, that it didn't matter what we did. He would just keep trying until he managed it.

Jonny was my best mate. We'd met three years before when his family had moved into the street. My house was at one end of the road; his, the other. We matched in several ways: dark hair, dark eyes and glasses. People mistook us for siblings. But one thing that didn't match was our ability to sing. While I could be outdone on a harmony by a choir of alley cats, Jonny had a voice like velvet. Every day he'd rehearse in front of the mirror, singing along to CDs, trying to reach higher and higher notes. With a tough home life, the thought of being on the stage was what got him out of bed every day. When his mother left the house for the pub, sometimes not returning until the next day, he'd bring us up to his room and practise. Sometimes you couldn't walk down the street without him bursting into song.

One day we were standing at his end of the street. I had a secret to tell him.

'I'm gay,' I said.

'Guess what? I am, too!' he replied.

It was a relief to find someone else 'not normal'. We were the neighbourhood's resident freaks – or so we thought. Walking through the area, day or night, was a bit like running over hot coals, except instead of trying to avoid being burned you were trying to avoid the local hoods, hoping they wouldn't spot you.

There were five of us: me, Jonny, Jonny's brother Jimmy, Big Gay Mick and Tanya, a sweet-natured English girl with long fair hair and blue eyes. But, as childhood friends do, we grew apart. Maybe we'd have grown together again if another ambulance hadn't come and taken Jonny away. His brother told me about it afterwards. It happened at a house party. With a few drinks in him, he'd got upset, disappeared and taken another lot of tablets. By this time his mother had been taken ill and was recovering in a home. Jimmy had been sent to live with his dad. The last I'd heard of Jonny, until Big Gay Mick knocked on my door, was that he was in a mental health hospital. Now he was dead.

I lived in the street for three more years. When I left, Jonny's house had been boarded up, the windows barricaded with sheets of rusted metal. The only window left untouched was the one at the top, the one through which the neighbours used to hear him sing.

When someone dies by suicide they leave behind questions. Attend a wake or a funeral in such circumstances and you'll hear them, posed by family members tortured by the big 'Why?' Why did she do

IT WON'T ALWAYS BE LIKE THIS.
IT'S GOING TO GET BETTER.

LYRA MCKEE

The journalist Lyra McKee, killed by a bullet during rioting in Derry/
Londonderry in 2019, pictured in a mural in the centre of Belfast
by the Dublin artist Emma Blake. The work is accompanied by words
written by the adult Lyra to her fourteen-year-old self.

it? Why didn't he talk to me? Why didn't she say goodbye?

Those were not the sort of questions that Mike Tomlinson, a professor of sociology at Queen's University Belfast, could answer. What he could do, though, was talk about the broader picture. 'Essentially, the story since 1998, which just so happens to be the [year of the] peace agreement, is that our suicide rate almost doubles in the space of ten years.' From the beginning of the Troubles in 1969 to the historic peace agreement in 1998, over 3,600 people were killed. In the sixteen years after that, until the end of 2014, 3,709 people died by suicide. Contrast this with the 32-year gap from 1965 to 1997, when 3,983 deaths by suicide were recorded. Over the last few years Tomlinson's research has mainly focused on one question – why?

'Now, that trend [the almost doubling of the suicide rate since 1998] is wholly out of line with what happens everywhere else,' says Tomlinson. He describes a presentation he gave at Stormont, the parliament buildings of Northern Ireland, that includes graphs of the trends in suicide in England, Wales, Scotland and Northern Ireland. 'Of all the presentations I've done in my career,' he says, 'there's an audible gasp from the audience every time I've done that [one].'

It's not that suicide didn't happen before 1998; it did, although researchers caution that it may not always have been recorded as such because of religious norms and relatives' shame. Yet during his research Tomlinson discovered that of all suicides registered in Northern Ireland between 1965 and 2012 (7,271 in total), 45 per cent were recorded from 1998 onwards. It's the oddest of anomalies. If the official statistics can be taken at face value, more people are killing themselves in peacetime than in war.

In a paper published in 2013, 'Dealing with Suicide: How Does Research Help?', Tomlinson wrote: 'Since 1998 the suicide rate in Northern Ireland has almost doubled, following a decade during which the rate declined from a low level of 10 per 100,000 of the population to 8.6.' The overall rate is now 16.25 per 100,000: 25.24 per 100,000 men and 7.58 per 100,000 women (2012 figures based on three-year rolling averages). In global terms this places Northern Ireland in the top quarter of the international league table of suicide rates.

Tomlinson identified adults who as children had lived through the worst period of Troubles-related violence (from 1970 to 1977) as the age group that experienced the most rapid rise in suicides in the decade after 1998. It seems obvious that this group, the middle aged who'd seen the worst of the Troubles, would be affected. But what about teenagers, people like Jonny? We were the Ceasefire Babies.

No matter whether we were old or young, war added new habits to our lives – everyday rituals that wouldn't be so everyday in most countries without war, like not taking your toy gun outside in case a passing army patrol or police mistook it for a real one and fired. Or watching your feet as you walked to school because the police were searching the area for a suspect device. Or getting hit by rocks that came flying over the 'peace wall' that separated us from the 'other side'. Yet those things were minor compared with seeing someone shot in front of you, as people older than us had done.

The Troubles' survivors would taunt us: how much had we really seen compared with them, even if we had grown up near an 'interface' where Catholic and Protestant

areas met? Yet of the 3,709 people who lost their lives to suicide between 1999 and 2014, 676 of them – nearly a fifth – were aged under twenty-five.

31 July 1972: the day three bombs went off in Claudy, a small village in the Faughan Valley, ten kilometres south-east of Derry City. That day Siobhan O'Neill's mother left her shop in the village, turning left to walk down the street. If she'd turned right O'Neill may never have been born. O'Neill never witnessed the carnage of the Troubles directly, but she saw its effects on people's everyday lives: in the fear of her parents when she told them, aged eleven, that she wanted to attend secondary school in Derry, not the village. Derry, like Belfast, was a hotspot for murder and bombings.

Today her job largely involves examining the legacy of that violence. O'Neill is a professor of mental health services at the University of Ulster's School of Psychology. In 2015 she led a team of researchers who established that there is a direct link between suicidal behaviour and having experienced a traumatic event, including those related to conflict. It was

THE MANY FACES OF THE IRA

Old, New, Official, Real, Continuity … since it first appeared during the War of Independence of 1919–22, the Irish Republican Army, or IRA, has split, folded and re-formed countless times. The organisation that conducted the armed struggle during the Troubles was the Provisional IRA. The Continuity IRA and the New IRA – the two main dissident republican groups currently active – were formed in 1986 and 2012 respectively. They see the peace process as a scam and believe that Sinn Féin, the largest nationalist political party operating in Northern Ireland, sold out or was, at the very

least, tricked, seeing Brexit as confirmation of this betrayal. Both continue to recruit – above all from the young, marginalised and drug or alcohol dependent (a survey in Derry/ Londonderry revealed that 95 per cent of young people see no future for themselves in the city) – and organise attacks: between April 2019 and March 2020 the Police Service of Northern Ireland recorded twenty-one bombings (including unsuccessful ones) and forty shootings. The main targets remain the police and the security services, but the strategy also includes punishment attacks (kneecappings, bombings and arson) aimed at suspected drug dealers and other 'antisocial

The Shankill Road (from the Irish *Seanchhill*, meaning 'old church') is one of the main roads in west Belfast. It passes through the predominantly working-class, loyalist district of the Shankill.

elements' in an attempt to position themselves as an alternative police force in the front line of the fight against crime. Despite the violence, the overwhelming majority of Northern Irish people, including Catholics and former Provisional IRA fighters, now see these groups as politically irrelevant, in contrast to the growing electoral success of Sinn Féin, and see the killing of Lyra McKee as a tragic example of the blind alley in which they find themselves.

Suicide of the Ceasefire Babies

Hands Across the Divide by Maurice Harron (1992),
a monument to reconciliation in Derry/Londonderry
signifying the putting aside of past grievances
to make a place for peace in the hearts of those
afflicted by the Troubles.

confirmation of what many had long suspected. Of the sample interviewed for the study just 3.8 per cent of those who'd never experienced a traumatic event had seriously considered suicide. If they'd experienced a non-conflict-related traumatic event (like a car crash, for example, or a loved one dying from cancer) that number jumped to 10.5 per cent. And for those who'd experienced conflict-related traumatic events? The number increased further still – to 14.2 per cent.

What shocked O'Neill even more was her discovery that out of the twenty-eight countries that participated in the World Mental Health Survey Initiative – including Israel and Lebanon, places with ongoing bloody conflicts – Northern Ireland was the one whose population had the highest rates of post-traumatic stress disorder (PTSD). Some 39 per cent of Northern Ireland's population, she says, have experienced a traumatic event related to the conflict. While suicide rates among the middle aged could, in part, be explained by the trauma of the Troubles, how could the death of young people who'd never seen the war be accounted for?

There is no single common factor in suicides among young people, according to O'Neill. Many things can be involved: educational underachievement, poverty, poor parenting. But the Ceasefire Babies are also dealing with the added stress of the conflict – even though most of them never witnessed it directly. 'When one person sees something awful, when one person is traumatised, it will affect how they relate to everybody else, including how they relate to their children, their grandchildren,' says O'Neill. 'People who've been affected by the Troubles live in areas where there are high rates of crime and poverty. When you're a child

growing up in poverty, being parented by people who've been traumatised and everyone around you has been traumatised, you are going to be affected by that, even if you've never seen anything. Even if they never tell you the stories.'

At the University of Haifa in Israel, students can take a course called Memory of the Holocaust: Psychological Aspects. Taught by Professor Hadas Wiseman, it outlines how the traumatic experiences of Holocaust survivors have been passed down to their children and grandchildren, a phenomenon known as 'intergenerational transmission of trauma'.

Much research has been published on the subject. In 1980 a husband-and-wife team, Stuart and Perihan Aral Rosenthal, presented their research in the *American Journal of Psychotherapy*. Titled 'Holocaust Effect in the Third Generation: Child of Another Time', it examined how the trauma of Holocaust survivors had travelled down the generations. It should have been a red flag to governments and policy-makers across the globe: the effects of war did not stop with the murdered, the injured and the traumatised.

In 2012 another study that looked at the Holocaust, published by researchers at the University of Haifa, confirmed what many academics had argued for years, that trauma survivors pass their behaviours down to their children. A report in the Israeli newspaper *Haaretz* (16 April 2012) said: 'Survivor parents were perceived by some second-generation children as being inaccessible, cold and distant. And even though these second-generation participants described their parents' inaccessibility as being problematic, some of them were perceived by their own children as being remote and cold.'

Researchers, including Professor Rachel Yehuda at Mount Sinai Hospital in New York, have been exploring how the effects of trauma and stress could be passed down to offspring biologically. Epigenetic changes – alteration of genes in terms of their activity rather than their DNA sequence – can be inherited, and it's thought these may explain how intergenerational transmission of trauma occurs. In August 2015 Yehuda and colleagues published a study of Holocaust survivors in the journal *Biological Psychiatry*, 'Holocaust Exposure Induced Intergenerational Effects on *FKBP5* Methylation', which revealed, for the first time in humans, that parental trauma experienced before conception can cause epigenetic changes in both parent and child.

These findings are among the latest in an increasing body of research showing that intergenerational transmission of trauma is not just a sociological or psychological problem but also a biological one. Could this heritable aspect of trauma explain why so many young people in Northern Ireland, like Jonny, take their own lives? As the sociologist Mike Tomlinson pointed out to me during an interview, the problem with answering that question is a lack of data. Who are these young people? What are their backgrounds? Where are they from?

Tomlinson recounted a time he was interviewed on the BBC World Service about his research. At the end of the interview a fellow interviewee from the USA asked him, 'Where is the evidence from other countries?' The problem is there's very little. In war the ruling government usually collapses and with it any form of meaningful record-keeping. Northern Ireland was unique: the Troubles was an internal conflict throughout which the

The road leading to peace in Northern Ireland began in the 1980s, but it took a decade of negotiations, some of them held in secret, to reach an agreement. The official talks were chaired by US Special Envoy George Mitchell, who announced on 10 April 1998 (Good Friday) that the United Kingdom, the Republic of Ireland and the main Northern Irish parties (apart from the Democratic Unionist Party, which would go on to become the leading unionist party) had reached an agreement, which was then approved by referendum in Ireland (with 94 per cent in favour) and Northern Ireland (71 per cent in favour but with big differences between Catholics, almost unanimously pro, and Protestants, who were split down the middle).

The founder of the nationalist Social Democratic and Labour Party, John Hume – the initiator of the peace process and its leading supporter for at least twenty years – and his counterpart in the Ulster Unionist Party, David Trimble, jointly received the Nobel Peace Prize. According to the accords the Republic formally recognised Northern Ireland's status as part of the United Kingdom, while London restored devolved government to Belfast with a complex system of power sharing. The definitive status of Northern Ireland was to be decided in a future referendum. The deliberately vague language used for some of the most controversial issues (demobilisation of the paramilitary groups, police reform, normalisation of the British military presence) meant that peace could be restored to everyday life, with the real resolution of these issues postponed until later agreements. From the very outset the accords were designed as the beginning of peace rather than the end of the conflict.

The Bogside, a republican area in west Derry/Londonderry.

'A sign outside the pub says: "No Topless Sunbathing – Ulster Has Suffered Enough". For tourists it's an introduction to the natives' quirky black humour, our way of dealing with all that's happened.'

state remained strong, even when Great Britain was being bombed. To borrow a scientific term, it's the best dataset we have to prove that the problems faced in a war-torn country do not end with the arrival of peace.

Yet the experiences of Northern Irish families in the post-conflict era are playing out in other countries, even if the patterns aren't being recognised. After one presentation at an international conference where he talked about Northern Ireland's soaring suicide rates, Tomlinson was surrounded by people from different countries affected by conflict. 'This is exactly what we see,' they told him. 'But again,' he says, 'it was anecdotal, it wasn't well documented.'

The Sunflower is a tiny little pub perched on a corner in the alleyways that sit between the edge of north Belfast and the city centre. With bright-green paintwork, it's known for attracting a genteel crowd of writers, journalists, poets and musicians, a smattering of post-conflict hipsters who wear tight jeans and tweed jackets and Converse. There are poetry readings and concerts by local indie bands in a smallish room upstairs. A sign outside on the wall says: 'No Topless Sunbathing – Ulster Has Suffered Enough'. For tourists it's an introduction to the natives' quirky black humour, our way of dealing with all that's happened.

For those of us who grew up in north Belfast and know the area, the sign calls to mind the suffering experienced on those very streets when a loyalist murder gang, the Shankill Butchers, drove around looking for Catholic victims to torture and kill. Yet one night I end up there drinking at a table with my Protestant best friend, at least two republicans and a group of Corbynite socialists. Times have changed. If I'd been born a decade earlier I wouldn't have dared venture down those streets, never mind drink there. Now it's safe.

It was there that I went one Thursday afternoon to meet Jonny.

We never figured out why Jonny's stepdad told Big Gay Mick that Jonny was dead. We found out within a day that he was still alive. Now he was sitting in front of me, toned and muscular, with his dark hair swept over his eyes, the glasses replaced by contact lenses. While I'd never really shaken off the unkempt geeky look, he looked like he could have been an extra in a *Baywatch* beach scene.

We'd all grown up together – me, him, Big Gay Mick, Tanya, Little Jimmy – but there was so much he'd kept hidden from us. While we were hanging out he told me he would disappear to his room and take a swig of vodka. Drink was easy to get where we lived, even without ID. Between arguments with his stepfather and mother, things had been getting tougher at home. The first time he'd tried to kill himself he'd walked down to his mum's, picked up a box of pills, swallowed a load and passed out while vomiting.

He'd had depression for a while. 'All I understand it being was sheer despair. It was a despair that you couldn't lift – it stayed with you all day, when you slept, and you woke up and you felt the same way, and you felt the same way when you went to sleep – if you did sleep,' he says. 'It's just a constant … I call it "the black dog". It's a constant sort of feeling hanging over you, of just pure "anti-ness", hopelessness.'

After a second suicide attempt he was taken to a mental health facility. Several more attempts followed. 'I was always very opportunistic – it was never planned out,' he says. 'If I saw an opportunity I took it, so I was quite impulsive, so it was quite frightening. I think I was under observation for a while.' Since then, though, his life had changed. With the help of medication to keep him stabilised he had his own flat and was going back to school. He still sang. He even planned to try out for a televised singing competition.

I was grateful to be there, in that weird hipster bar, drinking with Jonny instead of visiting his grave. Then I thought of all those who should have been sat there with us – friends and acquaintances who never made it into adulthood. We could have filled the Sunflower with them and still had people spilling out on to the streets. The problem hasn't gone away. On Christmas night in 2015 in Ardoyne – an area in north Belfast that saw thirteen young people kill themselves over a six-week period in 2004 – a young woman called Colleen Lagan died from suicide. She was the third member of her family to take their own life in the course of ten months.

Those who survived the Troubles called us the Ceasefire Babies, as if resentful that we'd grown up unaccustomed to the sound of gunfire, assuming that we didn't have dead to mourn like they did. Yet we did. Sometimes I count their names on my fingers, quickly running out of digits. Friends, friends of friends, neighbours' relatives, the kids whose faces I knew but whose names I learned only from the obituary column. The tragic irony of life in Northern Ireland today is that peace seems to have claimed more lives than war ever did. 🖋

Some names have been changed.

This article was first published in *Mosaic* (mosaicscience.com/story/conflict-suicide-northern-ireland) and used under Creative Commons.

In the UK and the Republic of Ireland the Samaritans can be contacted on 116 123. In the USA the National Suicide Prevention Lifeline is 1-800-273-TALK.

What I Learned on My Trip to Westeros

MARK O'CONNELL

A *Game of Thrones* tour bus parked at Larrybane Quarry, the chalk pit where Brienne got the better of Ser Loras Tyrell and Catelyn Stark announced the news of Robb's rebellion against Renly and his armies. It was also the location of the Kingsmoot at which the new king of the Iron Islands was elected in season six.

The TV series *Game of Thrones*, much of which was filmed in Northern Ireland, has given rise to a very particular tourist industry. When the Irish writer Mark O'Connell crosses the invisible border between the two Irelands and joins a tour of the series' locations, he sees how the magic of a fantasy kingdom is eclipsing the region's real history.

125

T he first time I saw a map of Westeros I was struck by how much it looked like an inverted map of Ireland. There were some differences, of course. Size, for one thing: Westeros is a sprawling continent, whereas the entire island of Ireland could fit snugly inside the state of Indiana. And the northern part of Westeros looked as if the island of Great Britain had been clumsily grafted on to it. There was also the fact that Westeros did not technically exist – that it emerged fully formed in the mid-1990s out of the volcanic imagination of the American fantasy writer George R.R. Martin – and that Ireland and Britain technically did, although their borders persisted in a state of ontological flux. My curiosity about this cartographic relationship led me to enter the terms 'Ireland Westeros map' into Google, where I learned that my observation was not an original one. Martin himself had confirmed as much in an interview at Comic-Con in 2014. 'Westeros began,' he said, 'as upside-down Ireland.'

Some time ago, long before I ever watched an episode of *Game of Thrones*, I became fascinated by the relationship between my country and Westeros. This fascination had its origins in a trip I made to Northern Ireland in 2017. My first book had just been published, and I was invited to do an event at a small literary festival in Enniskillen, a town about twenty kilometres north of the border with the Republic. Although the border is less than an hour and a half from where I live in Dublin, this trip to Enniskillen involved crossing it for only the second time in my life. My ambivalence towards the region was hardly unique: it is extremely common to hear Dubliners say that they have never been to Belfast, the next-largest city on this tiny island, and that they have no special sense of urgency about ever going.

Since the removal of border controls after the Good Friday Agreement, crossing between the Republic and Northern Ireland has been a frictionless experience. And there was, on that trip to Enniskillen, something about the nature of that transition – of being in one country one moment and another the next, and yet also sort of not – that forced me to consider the sense in which a nation is a work of fiction, an ongoing project of collective imagination. I found myself thinking often of the political scientist Benedict Anderson's description of

MARK O'CONNELL is an Irish writer, journalist and critic. He writes for *The New York Times Magazine*, *Slate* and the *Guardian* and has taught contemporary literature at Trinity College Dublin. His debut *To Be a Machine: Adventures Among the Cyborgs, Utopians, Hackers, and the Futurists Solving the Modest Problem of Death* (Doubleday, USA/Granta, UK, 2017) was followed by *Notes from an Apocalypse: A Personal Journey to the End of the World and Back* in 2020 (Doubleday, USA/Granta, UK).

'The region's status as "the home of *Game of Thrones*" was, according to the Tourism Northern Ireland agency, worth about $65 million a year in tourism alone. There were bus tours, walking tours, cycling tours, helicopter tours, boat tours, private luxury-car tours.'

nations as 'imagined communities'. (To be strictly accurate, what I found myself thinking about was the title of his book *Imagined Communities*: I was assigned it in college but got no farther than the cover.) And then, as I was waiting in the hotel lobby for a car to pick me up, my gaze was drawn towards a leaflet stand. Among the fliers promoting bus tours to various sites of natural beauty and historical interest, I noted one advertising a company called Game of Thrones Tours. The show films all over Europe, from Iceland to Croatia, but a majority is shot in Northern Ireland, either on location or on sound stages in Belfast. This company offered guided bus trips to the real-world filming locations of the show, which were dotted all over the pamphlet's little map.

I plucked one of these leaflets off the stand and, scrutinising the map, was struck by how Westeros had been superimposed over this troubled and ambiguous region of the island. It was an uncanny reflection of the process by which colonialism had redrawn the map of Ireland, and at the same time it seemed to offer a way of seeing the North that had nothing to do with its own dark and violent history. It was a way of being there while also being somewhere else entirely, of proceeding from one level of collective imagination to another, more fantastical and abstract.

*

Less than half an hour after the tour bus left the pick-up point, I realised we were no longer in Northern Ireland but had entered the realm of Westeros. We were passing Stormont Castle on the outskirts of Belfast. This was theoretically the seat of Northern Ireland's government. It was February 2019, and for more than two years at that point this executive office – jointly controlled by the right-wing loyalist (and largely Protestant) Democratic Unionist Party and the left-wing republican (and largely Catholic) Sinn Féin – had languished in a state of suspension thanks to a densely complex sequence of disagreements. The tour guide made no mention of this notable landmark, and the reason he made no mention of it, I further understood, was that it had nothing to do with *Game of Thrones*.

The guide – a man named Robbie, with a greying beard and a high voice – had appeared some years back as an extra on the show. This was one way in which Game of Thrones Tours distinguished itself: just about all the company's guides had some connection with the production. The region's status as 'the home of *Game of Thrones*' was, according to the Tourism Northern Ireland agency, worth about $65 million a year in tourism alone. There were bus tours, walking tours, cycling tours, helicopter tours,

The importance of a frictionless border to maintaining peace in Northern Ireland cannot be overestimated, and border posts were prime targets for nationalist attacks during the Troubles. However, the potential for violence lurked wherever there was contact between the communities in Northern Ireland. In 1969 the people of Short Strand, a Catholic area of Belfast, built a wall to defend themselves against loyalist attacks, a temporary solution that became permanent and was imitated in other areas. Some of these 'peace walls' – a misleading name, as an estimated 67 per cent of the victims of the conflict died within five hundred metres of one of these structures – are now tourist attractions, but they have not lost their original function and have actually increased in number since the peace accords. There were eighteen in the early 1990s, but by 2017 numbers had risen to at least fifty-nine, with a combined length of around thirty-four kilometres. That it is sometimes better to keep the communities separate is also illustrated by one of the triggers for many confrontations, namely the parades held by loyalist groups that are a bone of contention for Catholics (especially when they cross into their areas) because of their triumphalist nature and provocative attitude. 'Marching season' runs from April to August and peaks on 12 July, the anniversary of William of Orange's victory over James II, the Catholic king, at the Battle of the Boyne in 1690, which is celebrated by Protestant fraternities and lodges such as the Orange Order. Roughly two thousand parades are held annually, although many were banned during the Troubles and a large police presence is still required to prevent violence. Hurling missiles and insults at the other side remains part of the tradition, however.

boat tours, private luxury-car tours. In downtown Belfast there was a dedicated *Game of Thrones* escape-room experience. You could even visit the 17th-century Ballygally Castle on the Antrim coast for a *Thrones*-themed afternoon tea, where you would be served Littlefinger Mini Chicken Caesar Wraps and Kingslayer Cupcakes.

As we passed Stormont, Robbie was deep into a long and polished monologue about his experiences on set.

'They taught hundreds of us extras how to swordfight and how to die,' he was saying. 'I reckon I was one of the best at how to die, because I died seven times in one episode. At the Battle of Blackwater Bay I got shot in the back by a Lannister arrow. They changed my uniform, and then in another scene I got killed by a rock falling on my head. Then I got shot in the back again.'

Like some restless spirit who had taken command of the bus's PA system, he continued to cheerfully enumerate his many violent deaths and resurrections. Then the road began to run alongside a large body of water. This, he said, was the Narrow Sea, which separated Westeros from Essos to the east. In real life, he clarified, this was known as Strangford Lough, but for our purposes here what we were looking at was the Narrow Sea, and it was from here that we would be crossing to Winterfell Castle, principal noble house of the North and ancestral seat of House Stark.

When it wasn't starring as Winterfell on the show – with the aid of a little CGI enhancement – this estate was known as Castle Ward. I took out my phone, looked it up and learned that dating back to the 18th century it had been the home of the Ward family, local aristocrats; because of its symbolic connection to British rule, it was the site of a botched IRA bombing

The Fraser sisters – Kirsty, (headless)
Katherine and Amy – in Ballintoy Harbour,
County Antrim.

attempt in 1973 in which two people, one
of them a teenage girl, were killed when
an explosive device they were priming
detonated prematurely. Feeling suddenly
self-conscious, I angled my phone away
so that the woman next to me on the bus
couldn't glance over and see me reading
about the real history of the place. I felt
that I was somehow transgressing an
unspoken agreement to forget, for the
duration of the tour, the actual cartography of conquest and violence that
lay beneath the superimposed map of
Westeros. That was the thing about
Northern Ireland: knowingly or otherwise, you were always grazing against the
ghost of some horror.

*

I'll admit that this is not a particularly sophisticated view to take of the
historical and cultural complexities of
the region, but whenever I am there I
can't help thinking of Northern Ireland
as a place that has been no less imagined
into existence than Westeros, only more
thoroughly and concretely. Even before
the 1921 Anglo-Irish Treaty that ended
Ireland's War of Independence with
Britain and divided the island into two
distinct political entities, the province of
Ulster – comprising nine counties, six of
which now make up Northern Ireland –
was different, at least in a demographic
sense. It was the only one of Ireland's
four provinces with a majority-Protestant
population, most of whom were descendants of 17th-century colonial settlers
and committed to the country's union
with Britain. That distinction was a

major reason for the partition and for the decades of ethno-nationalist violence referred to, with rueful Irish stoicism, as the Troubles.

I experience the North as a realm of deep cognitive dissonance, beginning with the uncanniness of crossing a largely invisible border. I'll see the Union Jack flying from a lamp post or pay for something using pounds rather than euros, and I'll find myself wondering why everyone is just going around acting as if they were in Britain. The invisibility of the partition as an infrastructural phenomenon reinforces this niggling sense that some kind of collective fantasy is being enacted. If you didn't know anything about the context you could almost wind up thinking there was something vaguely whimsical going on, some gigantic and inscrutable performance-art piece that maybe had something to do with the fictionality of nationhood.

It was Ireland's and Britain's membership of the European Union that allowed for the dismantling of the hard border in the first place. And then came the Brexit vote in 2016, leaving us with an apparently insoluble problem. If Britain were to leave the EU it seemed that it would have to enforce its border with Europe. The prospect of customs checks and guards on the border between Northern Ireland and the Republic was kept at bay by the negotiation, in late 2020, of the Northern Ireland Protocol, which effectively located the border in the Irish Sea. But at the time of my tour of Westeros it seemed that there would be no way of

honouring the Brexit vote without reinstating a hard border, thereby reopening an imperfectly healed wound running athwart the Irish landscape and plunging the entire island back into the nightmare of history from which it had only recently begun to awaken.

Britain's decision to leave the EU was taken with little apparent consideration of this entirely predictable problem. It was as if, for the British electorate, the question was immaterial. Brexit wasn't about Northern Ireland – a region that, for obvious reasons, voted against it. It also wasn't really about the EU, or at least not only about the EU. You could say it was about Britain's vast and growing inequality and the widening cultural and economic rift between London and the rest of the country. You could say it was a democratic protest against the union's stultifying authority. You could say it was a reactionary fantasy, stoked by the right-wing press, of a great and ingenious people who had been hoodwinked into vassalage by a faceless bureaucracy hellbent on forcing Britain's fishermen to wear hairnets and introducing strict regulations ensuring the straightness of bananas.

You could say all of this and pretty much anything else you liked about Brexit, and it would not be untrue. And yet for all their complexities, both Northern Ireland and Brexit have a way of making plain the extent to which nationhood is bound up with fantasy. Despite the widespread tendency to think of them as immutable geopolitical facts, states

In 2003, after being wooed for a long time by the Irish government, Google opened its first European headquarters in Dublin's Docklands, the former port area beside the River Liffey. Ireland offered a flexible, educated, English-speaking workforce – but above all a new flat-rate tax of 12.5 per cent on company profits. Over the following years more technology firms set up not just in the area now known as Silicon Docks but also elsewhere in the country (Cork, in the south, is home to the European headquarters of twenty-four of the world's twenty-five largest pharmaceutical firms), specialising in tax avoidance through complex movements of money through subsidiaries, such as the so-called 'Double Irish' arrangement made famous by Apple and later replaced by the 'Single Malt'. At the cost of getting itself a bad reputation among its neighbours, Ireland's economy and government finances derived huge benefits from the 12.5 per cent rate, with tax receipts 'stolen' from other countries and tens of thousands of new jobs created, to the extent that in the depths of the financial crisis the government refused to raise the tax rate as requested by the IMF, preferring to cut the minimum wage and social security instead. But the gravy train could not keep going in the post-Covid-19 world, and after months of international pressure Ireland reluctantly agreed in 2021 to back the global tax reform put forward by the OECD, which will set a minimum rate of 15 per cent for multinationals to be paid in the countries in which they sell their products and services. Ireland estimates it will lose €2–3 billion ($2.3–3.5 billion) a year but still hopes to convince the multinationals to remain. Wouldn't it be a shame to leave such a lovely location in the centre of Dublin?

are structured on stories and sustained through acts of collective imagination. Over the complex and tedious reality of Britain's relationship with the European Union, Brexit superimposed, among other things, a fantasy of tyranny and liberation, a return to a great national past of heroism and glory. And this imagined nation was threatening to radically affect the shape of my own. Fiction, at a number of points, was exerting an existential pressure on the structure of reality.

*

'We now know,' Robbie said, 'exactly where we are.'

In a strictly technical sense we were standing in an earthy hollow in Tollymore Forest Park, about sixty-five kilometres south of Belfast, clustered around Robbie, who was cuing up a clip for us to watch on his tablet. But in another sense we were in what was known as the 'Wildling pit', where in the very first scene of the very first episode three rangers of the Night's Watch find the dismembered corpses of a group of Wildlings – tribespeople who inhabit the savage territories north of the realm. This was, in terms of *Game of Thrones* tourism, the holy of holies. It was the Omphalos of Delphi. It was the Church of the Holy Sepulchre. Maybe I was reading into it more than was warranted, but that, in any case, was what I took Robbie to mean when he said that we knew exactly where we were.

He held aloft the tablet in one hand and a Bluetooth speaker in the other, and a reverent hush fell upon the group as we watched the scene in the very place where it had been filmed. There, right ahead of us, was the tree on which the Wildling child had been impaled. If you looked closely you could see where the

One of the wolves who starred in *Game of Thrones* (taking the role of a direwolf), at the port of Strangford, County Down, surrounded by students from Arcadia University in the USA.

production crew had put a bolt in the trunk to connect to the girl's harness. And here, right where we were standing, was where one of the rangers was killed by a White Walker, which slaughter we were watching unfold on Robbie's tablet, allowing us to witness two realities at once, the real and the fictional. A sudden breeze stirred the birches above us, and there was an urgent whisper in the leaves. I myself didn't care much about *Game of Thrones* per se, and even I felt it, a numinous shiver running through the forest.

There were perhaps twenty of us. The group was largely couples in their twenties and thirties, a surprising fact that I chalked up to the centrality of binge-watching to the modern relationship. It was a fine day, clear and strangely warm for mid-February in Ireland let alone Westeros. We walked a narrow path alongside a river, clear water rushing over moss-covered rocks. It was all preposterously idyllic. But the beauty of this forest in itself was not really the point of our being here. The point of our being here was that its beauty had led to its being featured on *Game of Thrones*. There was a sense in which we could have been anywhere. There was a sense in which we were nowhere.

All of this – this situation in particular, the relationship in general between Northern Ireland and Westeros – made me think of Jorge Luis Borges's ingenious story 'Tlön, Uqbar, Orbis Tertius' (in *Fictions* by Borges, translated by Andrew

> 'Since the peace process, Belfast had developed a cottage industry in so-called black-cab tours of loyalist and nationalist neighbourhoods and of the elaborate murals variously honouring terrorists, hunger strikers, political prisoners, colonial conquerors and so on.'

Hurley, published by Penguin) in which the discovery of a fictional encyclopaedia from an invented world called Tlön causes the real world to give way beneath the pressure of the intricate fiction. In the story's haunting postscript, he records the flooding of the earth with the textual evidence of Tlön's invented history. The language of Tlön, he reports, is already being taught in schools, its 'harmonious history' already eclipsing the chaotic and bewildering history of the actual world. The appeal of Tlön, in all its imagined order and man-made coherence, is too powerful to be resisted. 'Almost immediately, reality yielded on more than one account,' Borges writes. 'The truth is that it longed to yield.'

'Tlön, Uqbar, Orbis Tertius' was published in 1940, at a time when Europe was consumed by a war of unprecedented scale and violence, but the postscript is written from the future vantage of 1947. For all that the story is rooted in a speculative conceit, it demands to be read as a political fable about the ease with which reality yields to the coherence of fantasy. 'Ten years ago,' Borges writes, 'any symmetry with a semblance of order – dialectical materialism, anti-Semitism, Nazism – was sufficient to entrance the minds of men. How could one do other than submit to Tlön, to the minute and vast evidence of an orderly planet?'

*

It was two weeks later, and we were in the cave where Melisandre had given birth to a shadow creature, and our guide, Brian, a wiry man with fervent eyes and a volatile wit, was talking about the varied quality of some of the other *Thrones* tour operators that were out there in the early days of the boom. One week he'd notice a guy on his tour taking photos and jotting down notes, and the next week he'd arrive at a location to find the same guy giving a tour himself, regurgitating Brian's material, messing up his jokes. Like his colleague Robbie, Brian took great pride in his stint as an extra on the show and the repertoire of anecdotes he had thereby accrued.

Since the peace process, Belfast had developed a cottage industry in so-called black-cab tours of loyalist and nationalist neighbourhoods and of the elaborate murals variously honouring terrorists, hunger strikers, political prisoners, colonial conquerors and so on. Many of the guides on these tours, Brian noted, were themselves former paramilitary members. It was his contention that a lot of them had sensed the change in the prevailing market winds and pivoted away from Troubles tourism to *Thrones* tourism. He himself had been in some borderline-hairy situations with these guys, he said. There was, for instance, an unpleasant incident a while back at

Before the partition of Ireland in 1921 Belfast was one of the wealthiest cities in what was then the United Kingdom of Great Britain and Ireland, part of an industrial triangle with Liverpool and Glasgow, and by far the largest city in Ireland. Over the course of the 19th century it grew from a population of 25,000 in 1808 to 385,000 a hundred years later, while the rest of Ireland was depopulated as a result of famine and emigration. The city's wealth was based on the production of and trade in linen (which earned it the nickname 'Linenopolis', just as Manchester was called 'Cottonopolis') as well as its shipyards. When the *Titanic* was built in 1912 the Harland and Wolff shipyard – whose twin cranes *Samson* and *Goliath* still dominate the city's skyline – was the world's largest, employing tens of thousands of workers. The port, the shipyard and the city as a whole suffered significant damage from Luftwaffe bombing raids during the Second World War, and over the following decades the shipbuilding industry went into an irreversible decline, exacerbated by the Troubles. In 1995 the derelict former industrial area occupied by Harland and Wolff was renamed the Titanic Quarter and earmarked for a major regeneration project, with residential areas alongside film studios (where *Game of Thrones* was filmed), university campuses, a bar-and-restaurant district and the world's largest museum devoted to the *Titanic*, which opened in 2012 on the centenary of the ship's ill-fated voyage. The museum delivered the desired 'Guggenheim effect', attracting more than 800,000 visitors a year (up until 2019) and becoming a showcase for the new Belfast, even though locals complain that only tourists can afford the ticket prices.

Ballintoy Harbour, the location for the Iron Islands scenes on the show. He'd been on the beach taking a photo with his tour group, all dressed up in cloaks and broadswords, and one of these new tour guides showed up with his own smaller group – plastic swords, chintzy cloaks – and asked if he could get in on the photo. Brian suspected his competitor was planning to use the photo for publicity on his own Facebook page and declined the request, at which point the man drew his gift-shop cutlass and challenged him to a duel. What seemed like a playful gesture, Brian said, was palpably the vector of a sincere threat. But he wasn't afraid of these men. If you'd done time on the set of *Game of Thrones*, he said, there wasn't much that could scare you.

Brian's guiding style was very different from Robbie's. For all I knew, it was entirely unique. Of all the consumer-facing tourism-sector workers I had ever encountered he was by some distance the most foul-mouthed. Within minutes of leaving the pick-up point that morning he was delivering an unexpectedly gritty monologue about the importance of punctuality with respect to the day's itinerary. He wasn't going to miss a location, he intoned, because someone had decided to take time into their own hands. 'I don't drop locations,' he said, 'I drop people.'

Nobody in the group seemed unsettled by this kind of talk; it wasn't hard to recognise Brian's hardboiled-tour-guide routine as high-concept, finely honed shtick. It seemed in any case unlikely that fans of a show notorious for its eye gougings and skull stavings, its lavish simulations of incest and rape, would be offended by a man swearing into a bus PA system. Whereas on the previous tour Robbie never referred to the actual history of violence that lay beneath the fictional significance of the locations – he was all Tlön, all the time – Brian had a habit of alluding to the reality of the place where we happened to be.

'I'm very glad *Game of Thrones* came here,' he said. The bus was slaloming along a narrow road, the glistening expanse of the Irish Sea to our starboard side. 'Before *Game of Thrones* my country was known for two things: the *Titanic* and the Troubles. The international perception was riots, bombs going off, blood in the streets. None of this was great for tourism.' Brian made a joke then about how the paramilitaries on both sides had handed in their weapons, and the *Game of Thrones* tour operators had swords now, and it struck me that there was something strange and even wonderful about the way in which real violence had been replaced by fantasy violence. This new dispensation was fragile, though, and contingent on wider political events.

The relationship between Westeros and our own reality goes deeper than mere cartography. In plotting his story, Martin draws heavily on the intrigue of the Wars of the Roses, a series of 15th-century civil wars lasting thirty years between rival claimants to the English crown. His invented world gets much of its texture from the real history of medieval Europe as well, although its dragons and assorted monsters are real and its politics vividly legible in our current time.

When *Game of Thrones* first aired in 2011 Barack Obama was midway through his first term, and, despite the recent global financial crisis, it seemed as if the technocratic international order would maintain its implacable composure indefinitely, that we were destined to remain in the cul-de-sac of history. The show, by contrast, imagined a world of Machiavellian scheming set against the darkening backdrop of climate change. It was also a world in which power and legitimacy were radically untethered, in which a former cohesion and strength had given way to decadence and endless crisis. If the show's success could be accounted for by a latent cultural desire for a return to a politics of violence and treachery, then the world had since received in abundance what it didn't quite realise it wanted.

For all the complexity of its motivations, the campaign for Britain to leave the EU also traded on a regressive and fantastical vision of the country's past: that of an indomitable island nation that had conquered the world, that had faced down fascism and that would never bend the knee to the petty bureaucratic tyranny of Brussels. The Leave campaign, for all its transparent fraudulence, demonstrated the potency of this ahistorical fantasy. It demonstrated the extent to which nations are works of imagination. The UK, in this sense, had become its own Tlön: an alluring invention imposed upon the darkness and chaos of an actual history.

*

In March my wife and I decided, more or less spontaneously, to take a trip up to Belfast with our son and our baby daughter, thinking it might be the last time we'd be able to do it without having to reckon with a border and all that went with it. My wife had never even been to Belfast. To our son, who had just turned six, we pitched it as a trip to the Ulster Museum, where there were dinosaur bones and ancient weapons and an exhibition of drawings by Leonardo da Vinci, with whom he had lately become obsessed.

I was aware of a certain tension

gathering in the gut as we approached the invisible partition, a tension that was unjustified by the crossing itself, frictionless as it was. 'Welcome to Northern Ireland' said the road sign about twenty minutes north of Dundalk. Someone had flung paint at the sign, five or six splashes, blood red against the white background.

'Nice,' my wife said.

At the time, things appeared to be deteriorating at alarming speed. A no-deal Brexit, until recently an unthinkable prospect, had become all of a sudden feverishly, luridly thinkable. That morning a document arrived in the mail from our motor insurance company – a 'green card' we would need to keep with us while driving across the border, which, in the event of a no-deal Brexit, would validate our insurance in the North. A couple of weeks before my first *Game of Thrones* tour a dissident republican group exploded a car bomb outside a courthouse in Derry. Shortly thereafter parcel bombs were found in London airports and a train station, mailed from locations in Ireland. It was hard not to consider a grim cascade of possibilities: a no-deal Brexit, a return to a hard border and an armed republican response.

On the top floor of the museum we came to a large and dimly lit room, more crowded than any other section of the museum. Its sole exhibit was a handwoven tapestry, eighty metres in length, mounted along the curves of a display wall. In the style of the Bayeux Tapestry, which related the history of the 11th-century Norman Conquest of England, it consisted of a seamless series of panels illustrating scenes of a violent history. A child pushed from a tower by a man with golden hair. A hooded figure savaged by a gigantic wolf as a woman with bleeding hands looked on. A knight beheading a horse with his sword. A woman in a cave, naked, giving birth to a creature made of shadows. These neatly delineated horrors went on and on, becoming more and more vivid as the tapestry progressed. (Luckily my son hadn't stuck around long enough to be subjected to these images. He'd taken one look at the tapestry, pronounced it 'just a big cloth going around the room' and demanded to be taken to the toilet on a lower floor by his mother.)

The tapestry, I realised, was now further along in the history of the show's War of the Five Kings than I myself was. I was midway through season two, having lately got into it in the most absurd manner possible: witnessing for the first time the beauty of Northern Ireland on those location tours, I wanted to see it transformed into Westeros. In recording the episodes of an imagined history, the tapestry was also a gauntlet of spoilers. What it really was, of course, was a clever marketing device, dreamed up by HBO and Tourism Ireland and made real by a group of highly skilled Belfast linen weavers. For every episode a new panel was added, so that shortly after the show's final episode aired, the *Game of Thrones* tapestry would be longer than the Bayeux Tapestry itself.

I didn't know whether I found the tapestry ingenious or horrendous or some volatile combination of both. But mostly I just couldn't discount the sense that what I was looking at was, in fact, some form of historical artefact, further evidence of the encroachment of the realm of Westeros upon our own. I arrived at the end of the tapestry, at the point where recorded history gave way to an uncertain future, and I thought again of Borges, of Tlön, of the way in which a complex and confusing reality yields to the man-made order of a

The ruins of a 12th-century Cistercian abbey in Dundrum, County Down, where Catelyn and Robb Stark received terrible news from King's Landing and Robb's standard-bearers swore allegiance to him as the King of the North. Here, we see Benjamin and Corinna McClune taking part in a *Thrones*-themed procession on their wedding day.

fictional world. Given the fragility of digital records compared with physical artefacts, it was possible to imagine future historians misunderstanding this cross-promotional tie-in as a real historical document. It was possible to imagine, in fact, that this would not be a misunderstanding at all.

I came to a scene of a banquet massacre, lavishly rendered. Throats slit, torsos pierced with arrows, a pregnant woman daggered in the belly. The terrible violence of the image was rendered appealingly neat, even pretty, by the skilful weaving. The red of the blood gushing from the wounds, pooling on the banqueting hall floor, reminded me of the paint splashed on the 'Welcome to Northern Ireland' sign at the border. Ahead of me a bearded man in his late twenties had been glossing each panel for the benefit of his female companion, who seemed less impressed by his historical knowledge than he was himself. He inclined his head now towards the woven scene of butchery. 'That's the Red Wedding,' he said, his face set in a performance of stern scholarship, 'one of the all-time great episodes.'

The woman said nothing, only nodded equably. It was unclear how interested she was in any of this. The world, I thought, was already yielding to Westeros. The truth is that it longed to yield. ✒

Citizens' Assemblies: Experiments in Democracy

The recent referenda on marriage equality and abortion that have transformed Ireland, came about through a democratic experiment, Citizens' Assemblies, which were established to help decision-making on issues that had been left unresolved by politicians for far too long.

URSULA BARRY

There was a celebratory atmosphere at the first Pride following the 'Yes' vote in the Marriage Equality Referendum.

Ireland has been experimenting with a different and innovative form of democracy over the past decade, namely Citizens' Assemblies (CAs). These have made dramatic contributions to social change in a country traditionally ruled by a highly conservative, repressive state, built on a deep-seated alliance between a right-wing populist political system and a particularly regressive Catholic Church. A culture of fear, shame, silence and criminality combined to suppress women's bodily integrity, their sexuality and reproductive rights and with equal force imposed repression, secrecy and hatred on LGBTQ+ communities.

THE IRISH CONSTITUTION AND SOCIAL CHANGE

Ireland has a written constitution, which acts as a framework for statute law, setting down key principles and rights that can only be changed by a majority decision in a national referendum. The Irish Constitution became part of the legal framework of the country in 1937, at a time when conservative Catholic ideology dominated political thinking and decision-making, and this was reflected in the constitution itself. A 'special position' was accorded to the Catholic Church, and the constitution included strict clauses on the 'family based on marriage' and a prohibition on divorce. Two highly sensitive and controversial themes have been addressed by CAs in Ireland: same-sex marriage and abortion. In an exciting and unexpected development, each CA voted overwhelmingly to recommend a referendum for change. The majority popular votes that followed in favour of marriage equality and abortion provision are unique to the Irish experience, and the results flew in the face of the traditional assumption that Ireland is a conservative Catholic country. A large majority of the Irish people voted in each case, and these changes were supported across all age groups, social classes and in both rural and urban settings. CAs have been both a driver of social change in Ireland and also a reflection of the deep process of social change that had taken place in the country over a number of decades.

It is important to highlight why these two referenda have been so groundbreaking. Homosexuality was illegal in Ireland until 1993 and only decriminalised as a result of a case taken through the Irish courts and eventually appealed to the European Court of Human Rights. Senator David Norris (a widely known and well-liked gay senator and professor of English literature with a focus on James Joyce at Trinity College Dublin) took a case against Ireland's 19th-century legislation that criminalised male homosexuality and which, ironically, did not even

URSULA BARRY is professor emeritus in social economics and gender studies at University College Dublin. She is the author and editor of essays that address feminism and gender inequalities, and publications to which she has recently contributed include *The Abortion Papers Ireland* (Cork University Press, 2015), *Economics and Austerity in Europe – Gendered Impacts* (Routledge, 2017) and *Gender Equality: Economic Value of Care from the Perspective of the Applicable EU Funds* (European Parliament, 2021). Since 2016 she has been the Irish representative on the EU Research Network on Scientific Analysis and Advice on Gender Equality and was a member of the expert advisory group for the Citizens' Assembly on Gender Equality.

'The Eighth Amendment reduced the rights of a pregnant woman to that of a foetus, bringing about a radical and negative reimagining of a woman's legal status in Ireland.'

recognise lesbianism. This British law, the Offences Against the Person Act 1861, not only outlawed male homosexuality but also abortion (defined as 'procuring a miscarriage'), and anyone found in breach could be sentenced to life imprisonment. That Victorian law was carried over into the legal framework of the new Irish Free State (later the Republic of Ireland) set up in 1922 following independence from British rule. Senator Norris won his case, and Ireland was found to be in breach of the European Convention on Human Rights in the case of *Norris v. Ireland* (10581/83 European Court of Human Rights, Strasbourg, 26 October 1988).

Ireland's anti-abortion law had, until very recently, one of the harshest forms of legislation dating from that same 19th-century law. It was replaced in 2013 by another draconian law, the Protection of Life During Pregnancy Act, which provided for termination only when a woman's life was in very immediate danger. It established a fourteen-year criminal sentence outside of such circumstances, which meant women in Ireland could only access abortion (except in the most limited life-threatening circumstances) by leaving the country, mainly by travelling to Britain. This harsh state of affairs was further consolidated after an extremely bitter and divisive political campaign culminating in a referendum in 1983 that inserted a foetal-rights clause known as the Eighth Amendment into the Irish Constitution. This clause provided for an equal right to

life between a pregnant woman and the unborn child she was carrying (despite the lack of any legal definition of the unborn child) and was incorporated into the constitution as a result of a major campaign by right-wing Catholic fundamentalist organisations. The Eighth Amendment reduced the rights of a pregnant woman to that of a foetus, bringing about a radical and negative reimagining of a woman's legal status in Ireland. This was seen internationally as a powerful declaration of anti-abortion sentiment by Ireland, prohibiting abortion in the constitution so that neither the courts nor the legislature would be able to liberalise abortion laws. Consequently Ireland has been on the front line of global anti-abortion organisations and represents one of very few countries to carry into law such a fundamental anti-termination provision.

In the context of such highly conservative social policy, the level of significant change that was finally brought about by CAs is remarkable. What was vital to this process is that the strong support for repealing the Eighth Amendment on abortion and introducing same-sex marriage established by CAs acted as a counterbalance to the rigidity and lack of responsiveness within the traditional political system to the process of social change. Despite the fact that Ireland was deemed to be in breach of the European Convention on Human Rights (by rendering homosexuality illegal) and in breach of the UN Charter on Human

Rights (by undermining the legal rights of pregnant women) the traditional political system appeared frozen or completely stymied by the conservative, fundamentalist right. The CAs have been able to break this deadlock within representative democracy and create a new impetus for change in a manner that has led many commentators to argue that in Ireland 'the people are ahead of the politicians'. That was seen to hold true by the scale of the vote both in favour of marriage equality and of repealing the Eighth Amendment.

**THE ORIGINS OF THE CITIZENS'
ASSEMBLY PROCESS IN IRELAND**

The origins of the CA process in Ireland lay in an increasing disillusionment with politics following the economic and financial crash in 2008, which was marked by an overblown property market and an unregulated banking sector that turned high levels of private (mainly banking) debt into public debt. Ireland was subject to a financial bailout by the EU followed by five years of extremely grim austerity policies. In this mid-crisis context a group of academic political scientists established the Irish Citizens' Assembly Project (ICAP), which gained ground very fast. ICAP secured funding (from Atlantic Philanthropies, an Irish-American philanthropic fund) for the establishment in 2011 of a pilot experimental project known as We the Citizens. The unexpectedly high level of support for the project is reflected in the way in which many mainstream politicians, who were initially cynical about this process of deliberative democracy, were largely won over to supporting it.

As a result of this changing perspective, the 2012–14 Convention on the Constitution was established under the

Every country has its own Ordinary Joe and Jane (Mondeo Man in the UK, for example), an imaginary stereotypical figure representing the average elector, and Ireland is no exception. But first, a brief culinary digression. Two sausages, two rashers of bacon, a slice each of white and black pudding and one or two fried eggs all stuffed into a baguette cut in half lengthways and generously buttered – with the optional addition of ketchup and/or a fruity brown sauce – and there you have it, a tasty breakfast roll, the traditional Irish breakfast reimagined for a modern population on the move. A full 1,300 calories, preferably to be consumed at a service station on the way to work the morning after a heavy night – a ritual celebrated by the comic Pat Shortt in his 2006 hit 'Jumbo Breakfast Roll' ('I don't have time for a fancy breakfast or put muesli in a bowl / I just head to the Statoil garage for the jumbo breakfast roll'). Breakfast Roll Man was the symbol of the Celtic Tiger. The economist and journalist David McWilliams, who coined the term in his 2005 book *The Pope's Children* (he was also responsible for the term Celtic Tiger), described him as the symbol of the Irish economy at the height of the construction bubble: the small-time building-trade subcontractor constantly rushing around at the wheel of his van. He was seen as the reason for the unexpected re-election of Bertie Ahern for a third term in 2007. Ahern, leader of the conservative Fianna Fáil party, was a backer of the construction sector but resigned a year later, mired in accusations of financial irregularity, as the Irish economy began to collapse.

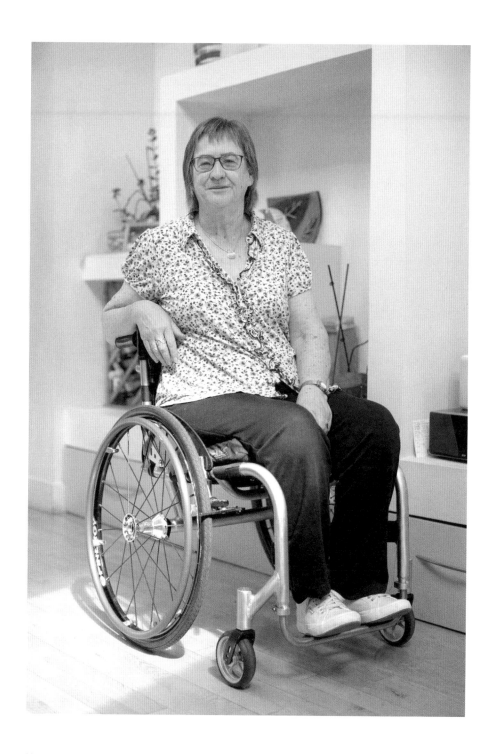

Ursula Barry photographed in her Dublin home.

Above: The former Fianna Fáil Taoiseach Bertie Ahern with his family.
Right top: Sinéad McSweeney, former consultant to the Ministry of Justice and currently Managing Director of Twitter Ireland.
Right bottom: A defaced election poster for the conservative Fianna Fáil party.

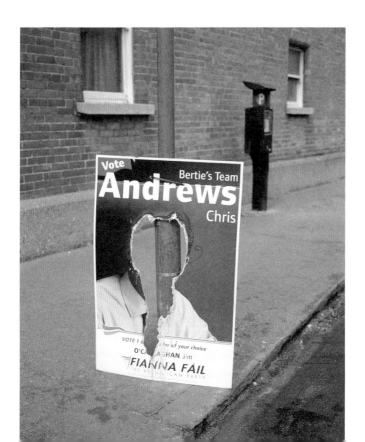

A group of young people stare through
the window of a Fianna Fáil club.

THE PASSENGER   Ursula Barry

2011 Programme for Government and was tasked with the aim of reviewing the Irish Constitution and recommending a series of possible changes encompassing different kinds of questions from the voting age, same-sex marriage, the role of women in the constitution, abortion, climate change and blasphemy. One hundred places were allocated in this convention, a third of which went to representative democracy (current elected politicians), two-thirds to selected citizens plus an independent chair. A key recommendation that emerged from the convention was to amend the constitution to allow for same-sex marriage, and the recommendation was implemented quickly and through a successful referendum campaign that took place in 2015. From a situation of criminalisation, of secret, repressed and hidden lives, within the space of just a couple of decades the Marriage Equality Referendum was carried by 62 per cent of voters, making Ireland the first country to vote LGBTQ+ rights into their constitution.

BEHIND THE SCENES

Following the success of the convention, 2016 saw the adoption of a new Oireachtas (parliament) resolution that established Citizens' Assemblies in law. CAs were now deemed to be made up solely of ninety-nine citizens (without elected representatives) and an independent chair coming together to respond to specific questions set down by the legislature over a defined timeframe of approximately one year.

It is interesting to look behind the scenes at how subsequent CAs worked in practice and how the decision-making and voting systems were designed and implemented. Citizens are drawn from a representative sample of the population on the basis of gender, age and geographical spread and willingness to participate. They receive expenses for participation (such as travel) but no other payment. The media are asked not to photograph citizen members during their deliberations. The process is facilitated by a secretariat drawn from the civil service and located in the Department of the Taoiseach (prime minister), an expert advisory group, a facilitation service and an evaluation process. CA gatherings hear a series of presentations and read sets of background documents from researchers, advocacy organisations, academics, lawyers and policy-makers. Under the restrictions imposed on live gatherings over 2020–1 because of the Covid-19 pandemic, the most recent, the CA on Gender Equality, had to be carried out online with significant backup and technical support provided by the chair and the secretariat. This created new demands on citizens to read relevant documents and watch video presentations online in preparation for each monthly virtual gathering, but this meant that the kind of informal discussion and exchanges associated with 'live' gatherings could not take place. By establishing a steering group from among the citizens and facilitating additional, more informal evening online sessions the secretariat came up with creative ways to ameliorate this, including Zoom polling and e-voting.

THE KEY PRINCIPLES

The main principle underlying the CAs in Ireland has been the selection of a representative group of citizens who then go through a process of becoming informed on a specific theme or topic through background documents, presentations, questioning of experts, and this is then followed by deliberation, using small-group interactive discussions and reporting to plenary sessions. Plenary sessions with key presentations and question-and-answer sessions are followed by intense small-group discussions and reporting back over successive weekends. This process creates the basis for informed voting on a set of recommendations, and government makes a commitment to consider each recommendation and respond fully to the Dáil (the lower house of parliament). Only plenary sessions are livestreamed; small-group discussions follow agreed guidelines about respecting differences of opinion, the right to speak to the group and to be listened to by the group.

So citizens deliberate on each specific question and, in most instances, vote on specific recommendations that are the outcome of that deliberative process. The preparation of the ballot paper for the final voting on the last weekend of the CA on Gender Equality in April 2021 was painstakingly carried out by moving between the group discussions and group reports to plenary sessions. The secretariat and the expert advisory group were on hand online with some additional legal and policy advice to try to craft a ballot paper that best expressed the thinking of the citizens. From the outset of each CA, the commitment made by government that each recommendation would be fully considered, encouraged and strengthened the involvement of citizens. Each CA built on the success of previous assemblies – the significance of the social change associated with those dealing with same-sex marriage and abortion had a marked impact on the levels of interest in the CA on Gender Equality, for example.

In addition to the work of the citizens in reading, listening and discussing each issue and potential recommendations, the public were invited to make submissions to each of the CAs, providing significant amounts of expert analysis and advocacy viewpoints to the citizens. For example, there were 1,200 submissions to the CA on Climate Change and 246 to the CA on Gender Equality. Higher numbers of submissions regarding climate change were a result of the CA seeking submissions from different key sectors, such as the transport, energy and agricultural sectors. In all cases the CAs received submissions from advocacy groups, professionals, academics and a large number of individuals, many containing recommendations for changes needed to legislation, policies and practices. Summary documents were prepared by the secretariats of each CA to highlight key points of analysis under specific themes and to indicate levels of support for different kinds of reforms.

THE CITIZENS' ASSEMBLY ON THE EIGHTH AMENDMENT TO THE CONSTITUTION: ABORTION

The CA inaugural meeting decided that the first issue to be addressed would be abortion, and the question of whether to repeal the Eighth Amendment (foetal rights) from the constitution would be the first subject of deliberation. Given the level of recurrent controversy around abortion in Ireland, compounded by the situation in which thousands of women were forced to travel to Britain every year to access abortion services in the private marketplace, this was not a surprising decision. The death in 2012 of a pregnant woman, Savita Halappanavar – who was seventeen weeks pregnant and going through a miscarriage in a hospital in the west of Ireland and was refused an abortion, despite her and her husband's repeated requests – had generated an enormous amount of renewed controversy, so public interest was intense. In fact, there was fear expressed that the CA process was yet another delaying tactic by the mainstream political system, which had refused over many decades to face up to the need for legislation for abortion services to be provided in Ireland. Once the process was established and the willingness of the CA to confront the abortion issue honestly and openly became evident, criticism receded.

Ninety-nine citizen members of the CA were selected as well as ninety-nine substitutes. Any citizens who withdrew were replaced from the substitute panel. Careful consideration has gone into every stage of the process of each CA to ensure that the citizens themselves were in control. Detailed discussion on the precise wording of every element of every recommendation that was to be included on the ballot paper took place, involving many changes, revisions and further discussions. Managing the time was all important to ensuring that citizens felt they had adequate scope to tease out each specific theme and that all views were taken into account when formulating recommendations. The high level of endorsement of each recommendation made by CAs reflects the scrupulous nature of this practice and the way in which a flexible and responsive process was built.

More than thirteen thousand submissions were received from a wide range of organisations and individuals, including many deeply felt personal stories, all of which were uploaded and personal profiles removed. Seventeen submitting organisations were asked to present to the assembly, including the Coalition to Repeal the Eighth Amendment, the Irish Catholic Bishops' Conference, Doctors for Choice, the Pro-Life Campaign, the National Women's Council of Ireland and Amnesty International Ireland. The final gathering of the CA on the Eighth Amendment passed a vote to delete the amendment and to replace it with a framework for legislation on abortion provision. This involved the CA voting on a range of different circumstances in which legal abortion would be accessed in Ireland and which was subsequently backed up by a Dáil committee recommendation. A historic vote to repeal the amendment was passed by 66 per cent in May 2017, a two-thirds majority comprised of all age groups, genders, social classes and geographic areas. This has resulted in groundbreaking abortion legislation, the Health (Termination of Pregnancy) Act 2018, which legalised and regulated abortion in Ireland up to twelve weeks' gestation (for any reason), and in cases of fatal foetal abnormality or serious health risks to the pregnant woman a more extended time period was adopted. However, the definition of fatal foetal abnormality is restrictive, and many women in these circumstances or who have passed the twelve-week cut-off point continue to have no choice but to access abortion services in another country. However, the CA, after decades of the most severe restrictions, played a pivotal role in making legalisation a reality for women in Ireland, many of whom could not afford or were not in a position to travel for abortion access.

What was fascinating in the two votes on same-sex marriage and the provision for abortion is how controversial both issues had been over so many years and the power of those strong majority votes in favour of change. In both instances it was evident as the campaigns evolved just how compelling were the stories of individual women and the lonely, shameful journey tens of thousands had been forced to make to access reproductive-health services. (One such poignant story is told by Gerry Edwards, a member of Terminations for Medical Reasons Ireland, of the experience he and his wife faced when forced to travel to England to access termination services, despite the fact that the foetus had a fatal foetal abnormality – see page 155.)

These accounts are also closely related to the emerging stories of unmarried mothers in Ireland trapped in mother-and-baby homes and in Magdalene Laundries – hidden, silenced, harshly treated and exploited – where high infant-mortality rates and hidden burials were common (see 'Institutionalised Cruelty' on page 27). So many women were denied access to their own children and subjected to the cruelty of systematic withholding of the records of tens of thousands of adopted babies by both Catholic and Protestant organisations. And there was also the power of the stories of gay men and lesbian women and their families and the way the traditional political, religious and cultural systems had marginalised and locked them out, denying recognition, cultivating hatred and undermining their many diverse experiences of sexuality.

GENDER EQUALITY, THE SUBJECT OF THE MOST RECENT CITIZENS' ASSEMBLY

The 2020–1 CA on Gender Equality faced very specific challenges because of Covid-19, which meant that after only one gathering of citizens, activities and events were restricted to online only. This was a complex undertaking, as it was not a single question (for example, in favour of or against same-sex marriage) but rather a spectrum of gendered equalities and inequalities that had to be documented across a complicated web of legislation and policies as well as the constitution. Many different questions had to be asked, and these were reflected in the high number of recommendations – forty-five in total – that emanated from the CA. Significant constitutional changes were recommended, including that gender equality and non-discrimination be deemed an underlying principle of the constitution, that the definition of the family no longer be restricted to the family based on marriage and that care and caring activities be valued and supported by the state.

Policy proposals were numerous and often linked to legal changes, such as legislation for the implementation of quotas to attain more equality in gender representation at all levels of political decision-making and within corporate, sporting, media and cultural organisations. Particular emphasis was placed on: the care sector and the need to improve conditions of both paid and unpaid care work; moving towards a publicly funded accessible and regulated childcare system; greater pay transparency and more flexible working arrangements and enhanced leave entitlements; a statutory right to home care and support for autonomous living for people with disabilities and older people; adoption of a fully individualised social protection system and a universal pension scheme; addressing gender stereotyping in education; adoption of stronger measures to address gender-based sexual and domestic violence.

An interesting feature of the CA on Gender Equality and the impact of Covid-19 is revealed in the open letter drawn up by the citizens that highlighted the urgency of recommended social changes and a rejection of a gradualist approach:

Tens of thousands of people celebrated on the streets
of Dublin on the occasion of the first Pride after Ireland
voted for marriage equality.

Megan Rankin, from Leopardstown, at a pro-abortion demonstration outside the Central Bank of Ireland in Dublin.

In recent years the citizens' assembly model has inspired a flurry of activity, particularly in Europe. The most active countries have been Germany and France, both on a national and a local level, while there have also been many initiatives in the UK. In general, by far the most frequently addressed issues are climate change and the development of solutions to cut emissions, reduce traffic and manage the ecological transition while limiting economic and social impacts. Alongside this theme, the German government, for example, sponsored two further assemblies, one on education and the other on an area that often remains outside of citizens' decision-making: foreign policy and 'Germany's role in the world'. In France, along with the climate, initiatives have considered agricultural policies and social cohesion, while in Canada the Commission on Democratic Expression has a three-year mandate to tackle online hate, discrimination and fake news. Wales also chose a laudable issue with its Measuring the Mountain project examining the world of social care, and Australia stands out for looking to the future with an assembly devoted to the legal, ethical and social consequences of genome editing. As with climate change, the aim is to set up a dialogue between science and citizens. On the same theme, there are plans for an even more ambitious initiative, bringing together citizens from all over the world in a global forum. On a local level, by contrast, various cities in Europe have involved their populations in discussions over the temporary challenge of Covid-19.

Covid-19 has highlighted a cultural shift in our attitudes to gender-based inequalities in Irish life. It has magnified many shortcomings and gender inequalities which are no longer tolerable. We want to see change now. We believe our laws and policies need to be transformed to make them fit for the post-Covid world.

(Open letter from the CA on Gender Equality, June 2021 www.citizens-assembly.ie)

INTERNATIONAL EXPERIENCES

Looking to the international experiences with CAs, the very first was set up in 2004 by the government of the Canadian province of British Columbia, followed by Ontario in 2006, to discuss potential changes to the voting system. Recommendations for amendments were put to voters by referenda but did not receive the requisite two-thirds majority. Today CAs are widely used at national and local levels in a number of countries, including Australia, the USA, France, Belgium, the Netherlands, the UK, Poland, Scotland and Wales as well as Ireland. CAs have been increasingly tasked with addressing difficult political issues. In many ways CAs have been seen internationally as a means of addressing democratic deficits in an increasingly globalised world where cross-national strategies are needed or where narrow political interests – notably around climate change and electoral systems – need to be bypassed. Traditional political systems have been notoriously slow to confront issues to do with the climate and environment crises, partly because they are international issues requiring long-term political and economic vision rather than the short electoral timescale around which traditional politics tends to operate.

CAs in France and the UK have been initiated against backdrops of political controversy or in situations of declared emergency. Protests in France (known as the yellow-vest protests) were linked to political upheaval over a proposed carbon-tax increase. In the UK the first CA was established in the aftermath of the Extinction Rebellion protests in 2019 following a parliamentary declaration of the climate emergency. France's CA was accompanied by a promise by President Macron of a no-filter process, which he described as a system by which policies recommended by the CA would be directly put to a referendum, to a parliamentary vote or implemented through executive orders. Drawing on a large budget, the French CA system has employed public-law experts, who were influential in shaping recommendations to meet existing legal requirements.

In the UK, CAs have taken place at both local and regional levels looking at issues such as adult social care in England, the future of town centres and congestion, climate change and the question of reducing greenhouse-gas emissions to net zero by 2050. Big questions on the future of Scotland and the work of the Welsh national assembly have also been addressed through CAs. In practice CAs in the UK have been more of a civil-society process, although the agendas for the assemblies were determined by parliamentary committees, which generated controversy from environmental activists and advocacy organisations who judged them as being too limited in ambition. Both French and UK CAs proposed hundreds of measures and recommendations that have yet to be implemented, but it is argued that public understanding and focus of the debate on climate change has been enhanced by this process. Climate-action CAs were primarily created in the hope that they could help break the logjam in the democratic process and effectively address global climate change, and more climate assemblies have been planned in other countries, including Germany, Scotland and Spain.

Ireland has set a unique example by using CAs in a much broader way to address socio-economic policies and legislation as well as core constitutional issues. Experience to date has seen referenda on significant constitutional change put into practice, but the broader legislation and policy arena has yet to be fully tested. The extent to which the diverse recommendations arising from the CA on Gender Equality will be translated into practice by enacting new policy and legislative measures is not yet known. Where CAs are seen to contribute to the democratic process, by adding an enhanced level of civil engagement and generating a new dynamic for social change, then they will be understood to have played an exciting and progressive role. 🖋

This is an edited version of an open letter sent to national public representatives in 2013 by Gerry Edwards, a member of the organisation Terminations for Medical Reasons Ireland (TFMR).

Dear Member of the Oireachtas

In October 2000 my wife and I celebrated our first wedding anniversary. Within a week we found out we were expecting our first baby. Imagine our delight - we would no longer be a couple, we would be a family. We immediately told our families and there was great excitement. At the beginning of February 2001 we went to Holles Street [the national maternity hospital] for our twenty-week scan and were taking note of crèches on the way that would be close to where we worked. We were projecting so much, where s/he would go to school, what would s/he do for a living, etc. I assume this is normal.

When we were having our scan we didn't notice the student ultra-sonographer leave the room or that the midwife had stopped talking and was concentrating on taking a variety of measurements from different angles. The obstetrician on duty, not our own, arrived in the room and took more measurements and eventually asked us to come with him. We were brought to a small room with soft lighting and a box of tissues on the table. It began to dawn on us that something was wrong, but nothing could have prepared us for what we were told.

It was explained to us in a matter-of-fact manner with a coating of empathy that our baby had anencephaly (we'd never heard of it) and that it was a condition which was incompatible with life (we didn't understand) and eventually that our baby had no prospect of life outside the womb - none! They were very sorry and there was nothing they could do for us in this jurisdiction.

We discussed whether or not to continue the pregnancy. It was made clear to us that none of the hospitals here could offer us a termination. My wife was saying she couldn't go back to work, she couldn't go to the shops, that she didn't want to go out at all, because she was obviously pregnant and people kept coming up to her and congratulating her, touching the bump and wishing her well. How could she respond? These people were well meaning and behaving in a normal manner, but every recognition of her pregnancy only served to remind her that our baby was doomed. The psychological toll was immense.

We arrived at the conclusion that the best thing for us was to bring the pregnancy to an end, and we could try again as soon as possible. We even went to see a psychiatrist and our GP just to make sure that despite our grief our thought processes were still rational. We eventually, through our own devices, managed to be seen for a second opinion in a UK hospital. There was no doubt, we were not talking about disability, which at this stage we were hoping for, but were talking about fatal foetal abnormality. Having discussed our options with this hospital we confirmed it was our wish to bring the pregnancy to an end, and we made an appointment for three days later. We left early the next morning feeling very much like fugitives fleeing the state.

The sense of betrayal, neglect and complete abandonment from this state is as acute today as it was over twelve years ago. As with so many people whom we have met and spoken with since who have had similar experiences to our own, we were treated with all the care and compassion in the overseas hospital that we reasonably expected from our home hospital. My wife delivered our son Joshua on 12 February by induced labour, and my mother-in-law and I were both present.

His birth, like other stillbirths, was greeted by silence. There were no cries, except for mine, my wife's and my mother-in-law's. I didn't look at my son because I knew of the extent of his condition, and I didn't want that to be my lasting memory of him. A young midwife took Joshua away to clean him and dress him in clothes a family friend provided and a baby bonnet that would fit a tennis ball to hide his wounds. We never even thought of clothes.

Afterwards a Catholic chaplain visited us at our request and had a naming ceremony. We couldn't get a Christening or Last Rites because he was stillborn. We similarly couldn't get birth or death certificates because Joshua was less than twenty-four weeks' gestation when he was born. My wife also did not qualify for maternity leave for the same reason and ultimately went back to work sooner than she was ready, although her employer was very sympathetic.

The next day we had to return home – without Joshua. My wife's father and my parents never saw their grandson. His extended family never got to kiss him goodbye. None of our family or friends were able to come together to recognise his existence and support us in our loss, which are all things that should have been able to happen.

Instead, Joshua was cremated alone in a different country to all of his family at a date and time we knew nothing about, and his cremated remains were delivered to us by courier in a cardboard box in a padded Jiffy envelope.

Neither of us had yet returned to work when the courier arrived, and I answered the door. My wife was still in bed but saw the van outside and knew what was happening. I could hear her wailing from upstairs as I signed for our 'package'. What kind of husband was I that I couldn't protect my wife from this pain? What kind of father was I that I couldn't even give my dead child a proper funeral, that left him behind in a foreign country and dragged his mother away from him?

I can never forgive this little country for having placed us in that position by denying us the right to bring forward the end of this doomed pregnancy here, and allowing us to grieve normally, to publicly recognise our baby and to have a grave that we can visit.

I have never been able to publicly write this before for a number of reasons - that I was afraid of public condemnation, even of physical assault from some; but mainly because I couldn't face recounting what happened, how I felt and how I continue to feel. I feel, however, that I must write this because so many mothers, including my wife, have shown such courage in coming forward with their stories and experiences and bringing about a much broader public awareness and understanding of fatal foetal abnormalities and what is being experienced by so many couples on an ongoing basis in a country of this size. Also, so few fathers have shared their experiences, possibly for some of the same reasons I hadn't previously, that this whole discussion runs the risk of being regarded as a women's issue when, in fact, it is a parent's issue.

The story of me and my son Joshua is not special. It is not a story you will have heard often, but it is not unique. It is shared to a greater or lesser extent by too many people and in the absence of change will be shared by too many more going forward. Have the referendum now! The government has probably lost all the members it would otherwise lose already. Don't make people suffer when it is in your gift to do the right thing.

Yours sincerely

Gerry Edwards

KEIRAN GODDARD

'It will not be long, love'

What does it mean to be born and raised in England but understand that Ireland is your spiritual home? Keiran Goddard takes us through a quarter of a century of his life, in which the passage of time has been marked by the lyrics of one of the most famous and heartbreaking of traditional Irish folk songs.

So, there's this song.

All songs are strange in their own way, but this one is stranger than most.

It's called 'She Moves Through the Fair', and it's a traditional Irish folk song. That means, among other things, that it probably isn't called 'She Moves Through the Fair' at all. At least, not always.

As is often the way with folk songs, its origins are murky and unclear; its name shifts and so do its lyrics. Sometimes the variations are pretty minor: alterations in tense, small differences in emphasis, a missing verse here or an added line there. Other times the song changes in ways that see it radically transformed: from a love song to an elegy, from a song you might hum while you were falling in love to something haunting, something cloaked in the thick, suffocating weight of loss.

In a sense this is unsurprising. Folk songs frequently exist in fragments, are endlessly reshaped in the telling, taking on traces of the communities, times and lives through which they pass. But even so, this song feels particularly unsteady on its feet. And maybe that's partly why I love it so much; it's a song that tells an elusive story, itself surrounded by elusive stories, shrouded in claims and counter-claims. A choir of echoes. It is ghosts all the way down.

It's probably a bit on the nose to tell you that I've been haunted for most of my life by a song that is both haunting and, in a very literal sense, about a haunting.

But it is what it is. 'She Moves Through the Fair' has followed me around for twenty-five years, and something tells me it will follow me around for another twenty-five, assuming I last that long, or the world lasts that long. It has been there while I grappled with my own name and my own origins, when I have loved and when I have lost and as I have slowly figured out what it might mean to tell unsteady stories of my own ...

1996 – My young love said to me / My mother won't mind / And my father won't slight you / For your lack of kine.

I am eleven years old, in my first year at secondary school, and things are strange. I have just discovered girls and masturbation and am spending practically all of my spare time cultivating these new hobbies. Everything else takes a back seat. The trouble is, most of the girls I am in love with are only interested in boybands and footballers. In people who are not me, basically. But I have a plan.

I use my pocket money to buy a Boyzone album. The girl I like most is obsessed with them, has pictures of them glued to her schoolbooks. They are a sort of Irish version of Take That but slightly softer, younger; more woolly jumpers and fewer leather chaps, more ballads

Left: Inside McCollam's bar in Ballymena, County Antrim.

KEIRAN GODDARD was born into an Irish family and raised in Shard End, Birmingham, UK, and educated at the University of Oxford. He is the author of one pamphlet, *Strings* (Antler Press, 2013), and two full-length poetry collections, *For the Chorus* (Eyewear, 2014) and *Votive* (Offord Road Books, 2019). His debut collection was shortlisted for the Melita Hulme Prize and he was the runner-up in the William Blake Prize. He is the author of a number of academic articles, speaks internationally on issues relating to social change, is a policy fellow at the University of Cambridge and currently runs a think tank. *Hourglass* (Little, Brown, 2022) is his first novel.

His might not be the first name that comes to mind when you think about Irish rock, but those who know his life story would not have been surprised by the results of a survey conducted by Dublin's Newstalk Radio, which crowned him the best Irish musician of all time, ahead of U2 and Thin Lizzy. Although he sold more than thirty million records during his career, which was cut short in the mid-1990s by complications following a liver transplant after years of heavy drinking, Rory Gallagher is known as an artist whose immaculate talent never quite gained the full recognition it deserved. Countless stars have paid tribute to him and his blend of blues and rock, from Jimi Hendrix and Eric Clapton to Brian May and Slash from Guns N' Roses, while his home town of Ballyshannon in County Donegal has dedicated a statue to him as well as a tribute festival that has been held every year since 2002. But in Ireland Gallagher is a cult figure and not just for his musical talents; it is no coincidence that his most famous release is *Irish Tour '74*, a live album documenting three concerts, which also feature in a film of the same name, that illustrate his love of the whole island of Ireland. He came of age musically in Belfast and never forgot it, not even in the darkest times when leading musicians avoided the city for fear of violence; undaunted, he continued to perform there at least once a year, earning himself the undying love of his audiences. As incendiary on stage as he was introverted in private and with little inclination for politics, he was nevertheless a beacon for the working classes, telling stories of people on the margins.

and syrupy cover versions. I don't hang about. I order a jumper from the catalogue that I hope will make me look like someone from Boyzone. It makes me look like a sad, gawky fisherman. I shave a line through my eyebrow, imitating the member of Boyzone the girl likes most. It makes me look like I've cut my head open and been stitched up by a particularly incompetent nurse.

The plan isn't a total failure, however. Because buried at the end of the Boyzone album, like a weird afterthought, is a version of 'She Moves Through the Fair'. I have never heard anything like it. It takes the top of my head clean off. It feels eerie and beautiful and every time I play it I cry like a baby. And I play it a lot. I play it in the morning before I get the bus to school, and then I play it when I get home from school, and then I play it again for good measure before I go to sleep.

It isn't a stellar version of the song. In fact, in many ways it's utterly terrible. Full of clichéd production flourishes that are meant to evoke something of Ireland's history of mystical poetic romanticism. But at eleven years old I don't know that. To me, it sounds like magic. Stuck in Birmingham, horny and awkward, with a ridiculous shaved eyebrow, I start to think about Ireland for the first time. About why so many of my family call it 'home' even though they don't live there. About my names (Keiran, Patrick, Duffy) and why I sometimes feel ashamed of them. About why I have never been to visit Ireland or even left Birmingham at all. About what the word 'kine' even means and whether anyone would really judge how worthy you are of love and protection based on how many cows you own.

Almost twenty years after hearing the song for the first time, I fell hopelessly in love and wrote a book about it. It was my first book, so, as is customary, I am now quite embarrassed by its earnestness. It opens with these lines:

The songs we liked
were the vanishing type,
simple enough to sing while we drank.
Nursery rhymes
about rivers and stones,
about wives, ghosts and fishermen in
      mourning.

Looking back now (through my fingers), I realise I didn't really mean 'songs'. I meant one song in particular. I meant the Boyzone version of 'She Moves Through the Fair'.

2008 – Then she made her way homeward / With one star awake / As the swan in the evening / Moves over the lake.

The banks are collapsing. I am convinced that capitalism is finally crumbling under the weight of its own contradictions. I am scared, but part of me is also elated about what might come next. Because by this point in my life I have learned that the world will absolutely judge how worthy you are of love and protection based on how many cows you own. This time we will build something more beautiful from the rubble. Won't we? Surely?

I am on a ferry to Dublin, and I am trying extremely hard to be moved by the sight of the grey water and the romance of being on a bloody massive boat. I am listening to the Sinéad O'Connor version of 'She Moved Through the Fair', which I have recently become obsessed with after hearing it on the soundtrack to the film about the Irish revolutionary Michael Collins. The film has been a gateway into modern Irish history for me, and now there are books and poems

and documentaries and a thick knot of feelings about what it means to come from an entirely Irish family but to have been raised in the land of the oppressor. Because I am young, and pretentious, and an idiot, I think of the River Liffey bisecting Dublin and decide ... That's me! That's my heart! That's my big, moody broken heart!

By this point in my life I am writing and playing music of my own. It is going fairly well, people seem to like the songs. But deep down I know it is not as good as I need it to be. I desperately want the band to be like the Pogues, but the reviews are starting to trickle in and they say things like 'overblown', 'pompous' and 'trying too hard', none of which are accusations that could be reasonably levelled at the Pogues. I'll carry on for a little while yet, but on some level the realisation has already dawned on me that I can't make the things I want to make.

On my last night in Dublin I am drunk, sitting in the corner of a pub while people around me take turns playing and singing songs. I want to sing one, too, but I am scared of being the twat with the English accent who gets the words wrong, so I stay quiet. Inevitably, hours after last orders have been called, the songs show no sign of stopping any time soon. There have been two renditions of 'She Moves Through the Fair' already, although the first singer calls it 'The Wedding Song'.

I have an early ferry the next day, and I know I should leave. But I'm terrible at leaving. And I also hate the idea that somebody might sing the song again and I'll miss it. But they don't. Nobody sings the song again.

I always stay too long.

2014 – And this she did say / it will not be long, love / until our wedding day.

THE PASSENGER   Keiran Goddard

An actual wedding day. One of my closest friends in the world is getting married. I love him and I am happy for him. During the service the bride's sister sings 'She Moves Through the Fair'. It catches me completely off guard. I've always thought of the song as describing a wedding that doesn't happen because the bride dies before the big day. I know there are other versions, versions that don't lend themselves to that reading; simpler, more joyful versions. But that doesn't feel right. Because for just a second it feels like everything is there in the song, the dying and the living and the being born. Absolutely everything. All at once.

The whole day is beautiful, practically everybody I care about in the world is here. But I can't shake the feeling that I am getting this whole thing wrong, that I am wasting my life. That all I really know how to do is drink and talk and I will never be able to make the things I want to make. The whole day is beautiful. But I am frightened.

2019 – I dreamt it last night / That my dead love came in / So softly she moved / That her feet made no din.

We all dress in black and put my granddad in the ground. Patrick, Paddy, Pakie. A thick-bodied man with elaborate red hair arranged to cover the fact he was mostly bald. I see myself in his body, in his vanity, in his politics. My family tree is complicated and splintered, with whole branches missing, so there are lots of people at the funeral who I do not know but who seem to have some sense of who I am, of who they think I belong to.

When the burying is done, the drinking can start. Funerals are cheaper if you have them first thing in the morning (the pauper's slot), which means everyone

SCOTS-IRISH

The huge Irish diaspora in North America is well documented, but there is a division within the community that is all but ignored outside the USA: among the settlers in North America (many made their way to Canada, too) in the 18th century, the largest group after the English were the Scots-Irish (or Scotch-Irish). They were pioneers twice over. Before setting off to seek their fortune in the New World, these Lowland Scottish Presbyterians (or their ancestors) had colonised Ulster in the 17th century with the encouragement of the British Crown. In the following century their hostile relationship with the Catholic community, hunger and growing tensions with Great Britain over trade caused many of them to move on and cross the Atlantic. It is calculated that around 250,000 of them emigrated, distributing themselves across many regions, settling new territory and often coming into conflict with Indigenous peoples. They were initially unpopular with the English as well but redeemed themselves by playing a key role in the American War of Independence, to the extent that they came to embody the American ideal in terms of their determination, patriotic zeal and entrepreneurial spirit. They helped to found both the Republican and Democratic parties along with many educational institutions with religious origins, such as the future Princeton University. But their legacy still remains controversial, and they have also been accused of dogmatic moralism and racism and criticised for their involvement in the slave trade. No one at first referred to them as Scots-Irish, but in the 19th century they applied the name to themselves to emphasise their roots and so distinguish themselves from a new wave of Irish immigrants, Catholic this time, who were fleeing the Famine.

is four drinks deep before lunchtime. We are all gathered in a local Irish club, which is essentially just a dark room with an especially melancholy jukebox. There aren't nearly enough of us to make the place feel full. For some reason I feel responsible for this and start negotiating with the barman about whether he can close off part of the room so that it feels less empty.

By early afternoon things feel better, looser, easier. And then something beautiful happens. An extremely old man comes into the club with his extremely old wife. Between them they are wheeling an upright piano, slowly and awkwardly, into the corner of the room. I go over to talk to them and ask how they knew my grandad. But they didn't know him. They just live down the road and like to bring their piano along whenever there is an Irish wake or an Irish wedding in case anyone wants to hear them play a song: 'Any of the old songs, we know them all, just get us a drink and we'll play whatever you like.'

It's obvious what song I ask them to play. And they play it.

At the end of the evening I meet four of my grandad's sisters. I didn't even know he had sisters. They tell me stories about growing up together in County Monaghan, on a small farm in the heart of the border counties. One of their cousins was a famous local poet, they tell me, who wrote poems about God and nature for the local paper. They'll send me some photocopies from their scrapbook, they say. And some pictures of their grandchildren and of their grandchildren's children.

2021 – She went away from me and she moved through the fair / Where hand-slapping dealers' loud shouts rent the air.

The world has gone quiet. There is a sickness in the air, and it has shut us all into our homes. The only crowds left are angry crowds. Angry at the police, angry at the government, angry about occupations and terror that we watch helplessly unfold and persist ... and persist ... and persist ... and persist ... through the screens of our phones.

Today London is flooded and alive with the flag of Palestine. With the gift of solidarity. With the only real gift there is.

And there are Irish flags, too. Irish flags and placards dotted across Victoria Embankment, as far as the eye can see. The one directly in front of me reads *... Saoirse don Phalaistín – One struggle.* Seeing it does something to me that is hard to explain. But it is something like what 'She Moves Through the Fair' did to me that first time, twenty-five years ago.

Haunted. No longer ashamed of my name. But still scared. That I will never make the things I want to make. Because I always stay too long. Because all I am good at is drinking and talking. Because I never go home.

And because there is an email I will never reply to. An email full of poems about God and nature, clipped out of the local paper. Full of pictures of people I do not know and will probably never meet.

My phone feels heavy in my back pocket.

It is ghosts all the way down. 🖋

Irish Rugby Is Different

A line-out between Lansdowne FC
(in black, red and yellow) and Clontarf
during a Metropolitan Cup match held
at Clontarf Rugby Club in Dublin.

Rugby is a hugely popular sport in Ireland and occupies a special position: it is not divided by the religious and political fault lines between north and south, unionist and republican, and the national rugby union team is the only one to represent the whole of the island – but a class barrier remains in place that can determine whether or not a child will ever actually play the game.

BRENDAN FANNING

TWO COUNTRIES, ONE NATIONAL TEAM

In the build-up to the 1987 Rugby World Cup in New Zealand, the first rugby union tournament of its kind (here and throughout this article we are talking about the sport of rugby union rather than rugby league), the Ireland squad had a training session at a Dublin club under coach Mick Doyle. The players were travelling from various parts of the island and were due on the field at Merrion Road, ready to go, by mid-morning.

Ireland draws almost all its players from its four historical provinces: Connacht, Leinster, Munster and Ulster. Most of Ulster is in Northern Ireland, however, part of the UK. In this Ireland squad there were ten men from Ulster. Two of them, Jimmy McCoy and John McDonald, were policemen with the Royal Ulster Constabulary (RUC) – the police force in Northern Ireland at the time – which, being considered a unionist organisation by many republicans, was a top target for the IRA, so whenever McDonald and McCoy came south to play for Ireland they would be shadowed by An Garda Síochána, the police on the Republic of Ireland side of the border. It was inconvenient, but it worked. There had never been any trouble on rugby duty.

On the day of this squad session, however, there were a few no-shows. Ulster players David Irwin, Nigel Carr and Philip Rainey were travelling together from Belfast. Everything was fine until they were approaching the border. At the same time, travelling in the opposite direction, were a Northern Irish judge and his wife, Lord Justice Gibson and Lady Gibson. Judges were also on the IRA hit list. A 500-pound bomb had been planted in a parked car a few miles in from the northern side of the border, and it was detonated remotely as the Gibsons passed by. They were killed instantly. The three Ireland players – Irwin, Carr and Rainey – were heading in the other direction and were blown off the road. All three survived, but Carr would never recover from his injuries sufficiently to resume his rugby career.

The tragedy highlighted the unique nature of Irish rugby. No other country going to that first World Cup could identify with the problems of having players from two different countries – one group living daily under the threat of terrorism – playing under the same flag. No other rugby nation had issues with the flag they played under. No other rugby nation had issues with the anthem played while the team stood to attention before that flag on match day.

Ireland played Wales in the opening game of their World Cup campaign. In the lead-up it emerged they would be the only team in the tournament with no anthem to play before kick-off. Because the team had players from two jurisdictions they played 'Amhrán na bhFiann', the anthem of the Republic, for home games at Dublin's Lansdowne Road and nothing at all when playing away in the Five Nations Championship (an annual competition between England, Scotland, Ireland,

BRENDAN FANNING has been involved in rugby his whole life, as a player, a coach and a journalist. His book *From There to Here: Irish Rugby in the Professional Era* (Gill & Macmillan, 2007) is considered the definitive text on the metamorphosis of Irish rugby union from an amateur to a professional sport. He also collaborated with Irish rugby legend Willie Anderson on the latter's autobiography, *Crossing the Line: The Flag, the Haka and Facing My Life* (Reach Sport, 2021). He has been a sports correspondent for Ireland's *Sunday Independent* newspaper since 1996.

Wales and France that became the Six Nations in 2000 when Italy joined). But a World Cup, the first of its kind, and no one had thought of coming up with a piece of music that suited people on both sides of the Irish border?

Team captain Donal Lenihan was horrified to discover his men would be at a loss before the game even started. 'When I saw the other teams in the tournament taking such pride in and giving such passion to their anthems, I just felt we were missing out,' he wrote in his autobiography *My Life in Rugby* (Transworld Ireland, 2016). 'I was motivated by the right reasons, even if the end result proved embarrassing – for which I must take responsibility.'

What had happened was that under time pressure to fill the void – and with Lenihan trying to find a solution – they ended up using a version of the popular Irish ballad 'The Rose of Tralee' crackling over the PA system. In the rush to find a suitable recording the management had borrowed from one of the players a copy of an album featuring the song by big-band leader James Last.

Tommy Bowe was just fifteen years old in 1999, but the former Irish rugby union international vividly remembers the first European trophy win for an Irish club, when Ulster beat French outfit Colomiers at Dublin's historic Lansdowne Road stadium to win the Heineken Cup. He describes how wonderful it was to hear of fans from all over Ireland, including those from rivals like Leinster and Munster, coming to the capital to support Ulster. At club level this was the first time it had happened. Tommy was born 'five minutes away' from the border with Ulster in County Monaghan. 'I went to primary school in Ireland and secondary school in Northern Ireland. My mum worked over the border in a hospital. For us it was completely normal to deal with the checkpoints. I regularly played against Northern Irish teams. I got to realise that there was no difference between the two sides.' Tommy started playing in his home country but carried on at the Royal School, Armagh in Northern Ireland and went to Belfast University, so it was no real surprise that he turned professional with Ulster, the Belfast side that was seen as a symbol of unionism at the time. 'Nowadays the players in the Irish teams are organised centrally as a federation, and many others have taken the path I did, although I was probably one of the first. It was a brilliant pathway. Thanks to rugby I feel a part of both sides and I'm happy to represent unity. Sport brings people together.' He won the Six Nations twice with Ireland (2009 and 2015), and in 2010 he was voted player of the championship and is the all-time third-highest try scorer for the Irish national team. (Federico Meda)

The Lansdowne FC club building with the Aviva Stadium behind it.
The Aviva Stadium is used as their home ground by both the Ireland
rugby union side and the Republic of Ireland football team.

Last's chart-topping success was based on his trademark 'happy music' – and it was an awful choice. Mortified by the compromise, the Irish players went back to having no anthem for the remaining games in the tournament, missing out on something all of their opponents valued as part of their warm-up.

The fiasco caused a huge debate at the time. Typically, however, it took the Irish Rugby Football Union (IRFU) almost eight more years to commission songwriter Phil Coulter to come up with a solution. By the time they went to the World Cup in South Africa in 1995 they had something that worked for both north and south, 'Ireland's Call'. Still there was a twist, however. Over the years many Ulster players had struggled with having to stand to attention for 'Amhrán na bhFiann', so when Ireland play at home they get two songs, 'Amhrán na bhFiann' *and* 'Ireland's Call', but when they play away they get just the one, 'Ireland's Call'.

Ireland is different.

This difference was brought home with force again two years after that 1987 World Cup. This time it was Ireland against New Zealand at Lansdowne Road. More than four million people have watched the YouTube clip of Ireland captain Willie Anderson challenging the New Zealand All Blacks as they performed the *haka*, the war dance they use so effectively to prime themselves for the battle to come. He was determined not to let New Zealand come into Ireland's back yard and win over the

crowd before a ball had even been kicked. It was an incredible few moments that had 48,000 people on their feet as Anderson and his players, arms linked, marched into the middle of the *haka*. He ended up almost nose to nose with New Zealand captain Buck Shelford. As Anderson said afterwards, 'New Zealand won the game; we won the dance!'

As captain it was Anderson's duty to speak at the banquet that night. He thanked the usual people and spoke about the atmosphere just before kick-off and how at the time it felt like the most important thing in the world – a life-or-death situation. But it wasn't. After the game Anderson had been taken aside and told of the death in Northern Ireland of a good friend of his, another victim of terrorism. The news had been kept from him when he was in the Ireland camp.

'We play rugby as if our lives depend on it, which feels right at the time,' he said in his speech. 'But real life is going on beyond the pitch. Real life for me is the death of my friend Bob Glover, blown up by the IRA a couple of days ago, and I'd like to pay tribute to a good man tonight.'

Anderson's friend was just thirty-seven, an officer in the Ulster Defence Regiment; being a regiment of the British Army the UDR were, like the RUC, prime targets for the IRA. He left a wife and three children, one of whom would marry Anderson's son many years later. On the night of the game the All Blacks commiserated with Anderson on his loss. They couldn't understand that players based in Ulster had this level of threat so close at hand. The IRFU, however, were already angry with their captain for challenging the *haka*, and this was compounded by bringing the political situation in the island into his speech at the banquet.

Ireland is definitely different.

THE RO'CK

In January 1998 Ross O'Carroll-Kelly was born, delivered on the sports desk of the *Sunday Tribune*. The newspaper is now long gone, but Ross is still alive and kicking. Total sales of his twenty-three books passed the million mark a couple of years ago. There have been four stage productions and countless newspaper columns.

He was conceived by Paul Howard, who is still churning out words on the character, and Ger Siggins, who was the sports editor of the *Tribune*. The whole thing began as a few paragraphs in a general, light-hearted column on sport, then it became the diary of a fictional schools-rugby player. Then it developed into an Irish phenomenon.

The name Ross O'Carroll-Kelly ticked a number of boxes: first, it is double-barrelled, which was a growing trend in Ireland at the time of his conception; second, the acronym spells ROCK, which is the common abbreviation for the top rugby-playing private school Blackrock College, the biggest and best-known of its kind in the country. Howard had covered plenty of schools rugby in his early years as a journalist. Coming from a working-class background himself – football and boxing were his first loves – the rituals associated with the Leinster Schools Senior Cup (largely played by teams from fee-paying schools; see 'Rugby in Ireland' on page 175) were alien to him. With rugby he came face to face with a sport that obsessed a swathe of middle-class people in south County Dublin. One thing that particularly struck him at these schools games was those dads who were still living out their sporting dreams through their sons, and the lightbulb moment for the creation of the character came when Howard received a solicitor's letter from an angry parent because in one of his match reports a crucial try had been accredited to the wrong boy. Could this really be happening?

The columns featuring the fictional private-school rugby-playing jock Ross started out as a way of satirising the schools-rugby community, which takes itself very seriously, but the people Howard was poking fun at actually loved the attention. They could see themselves in the characters and the stories. This was their private-school world, and they enjoyed a spotlight being shone upon it.

'A friend of mine who worked in a bookshop told me that these kids used to come in on a Saturday morning, and it'd be like five of them crowded around the books, laughing and saying, "Oh, that's so Traolach" [Traolach being an Irish first name that might be given to children of wealthier families who don't speak the Gaelic language but wish to appear as if they do],' Howard said in an interview in the *Irish Times* on 26 January 2021. 'And this was so disappointing to me because Ross was really born out of my class consciousness and my sense that, you know, if you had money in Ireland that you could lead a largely frictionless life … [Although] what I've realised, especially over the last two or three years writing the books, is that Ross is now probably the only character in the books that I really love. And at the very beginning, I set out to make him the most hateful character in the books.' The worse Ross's behaviour got, the more he showed himself to be tone deaf, the faster the books flew off the

The Clontarf coach and spectators watching a match at Clontarf Rugby Club, Dublin.

shelves. Ross O'Carroll-Kelly became the ambassador for schools-rugby lovers in a wealthy pocket of the nation's capital city.

IRISH RUGBY'S SOCIAL DIVIDE

If the political north–south divide on the island of Ireland is hard to miss then there is also another divide. This one doesn't involve terrorism or fundamental differences over flags and anthems, but there are two separate identities: boys who go to fee-paying schools and play rugby and those who go to non-fee-paying schools and play Gaelic games or football.

Of course, there is a crossover, but the Irish rugby model has traditionally relied on what the private schools brought to the table. It is a very small base. The picture has changed somewhat over the years, but still the divide is obvious. For example, when Ireland played Italy in the Six Nations Championship in February 2021, thirteen players in the

Irish squad came up through private schools, five through non-fee-paying schools and the remaining five were developed in New Zealand, South Africa or England. Go back ten years to when the countries met in the 2011 World Cup, and the picture was similar: fifteen from private schools, six from non-fee-paying schools and one from Australia (the match-day squad was twenty-two at the time). So over that decade the IRFU had not made much headway in broadening their social base, and Irish rugby still revolves around a small patch of south County Dublin, home to Blackrock College and St Michael's College – the principal nurseries for the professional game. Leinster, which includes County Dublin, has been the dominant province in Irish rugby for the last ten years (for more on the way rugby is organised in the country see 'Rugby in Ireland' on page 175). Of Leinster Rugby's current forty-seven-man senior squad, eighteen went to either Blackrock or St Michael's. It's remarkable these schools are so good at developing talent. And it's equally remarkable rugby's footprint is so small both socially and geographically.

Breaking the mould, however, is Tadhg Furlong, one of the top names in the current Leinster squad. Twice a British and Irish Lion – a touring team chosen from the top players in England, Ireland, Scotland and Wales – he is one of the best tight-head props in the world. Furlong – a Gaelic football player originally – is from County Wexford, a long, long way culturally from the rich rugby belt of County Dublin, but he was good enough to be spotted playing youth rugby with the junior club New Ross and to get a sought-after place at the prestigious Leinster Rugby Academy.

'I left school at seventeen,' he said in

Clontarf Rugby Club players during a training session.

THE PASSENGER   Brendan Fanning

an interview in the *Irish Independent* (30 September 2018), in which he described the transition from Wexford to the bright lights of the capital. 'I came up to Dublin. I won't lie: my first night up in Dublin, I was ringing up my mother and asking how to cook pasta. What do I do here? It's kind of hard to project yourself back to what type of state of mind you were in. I suppose I was taking a shot into the unknown really because there was always such a thing within the youths' system about all of the schools lads, and you never know how you compare or where you stand or the standard of these guys because you never see them.

'I don't know if the [Leinster Schools Rugby] Senior Cup was on TV back then, but if it was, we probably didn't have the channel to watch it. You see these lads who are a bit ahead of you on the development ladder, and I suppose you have that bit of a chip on your shoulder, that you need to get stuck in there.

'Let's not be naive here. I was raw leaving school. I had never really touched weights. With all of the goodness in my heart to New Ross RFC [rugby football club], we trained one night a week in my final year there and played at the weekend, so from a skills-based game knowledge/game appreciation and from the point of view of my strength-and-condition profile, I was way behind the eight ball.'

Furlong developed to a point where he could clear the table, however. But every time a player like him comes through the youths' system and not the private schools the tendency is to presume the system is running smoothly. It's not. In a country as small as Ireland it is sheer madness not to challenge the tradition aggressively and convert players from outside the world of private schools.

RUGBY IN IRELAND

The world of Irish rugby union is divided into four administrative units: Leinster, the focal point for Greater Dublin; Munster for the south (Cork, Limerick and Shannon); Connacht for Galway (the west coast); and, finally, Ulster for the north. Before 1990 the year the All Ireland League was founded, each branch organised its own independent championship, and this is why the Schools Rugby Senior Cup competitions, which still follow the same geographical divisions, have never lost their appeal. Dating back to the 19th century, the finals of these school tournaments are normally played during the week of St Patrick's Day, attracting huge crowds hoping to see 'the next big thing'. The Leinster Schools Senior Cup, which attracts the largest following, even goes out live on TV. These historic geographical divisions were also maintained after the transition to the professional game in 1995, as it proved useful to sign up each branch to the Celtic League (2001), in which they played regular games against their Scottish and Welsh counterparts. They were then joined by Italian and South African sides in 2009 and 2017 respectively. The tournament is now known as the United Rugby Championship and has expanded to sixteen teams. This experiment with a transnational (and intercontinental) league has not always worked well: some teams have been disbanded or replaced, others have gone bankrupt. The only union never to have changed anything is Ireland, and an Irish side has topped the championship thirteen years out of twenty. Leinster holds the record with eight titles, but Ireland also boasts another record: it is the only nation in which every team has won at least one title (Munster three, Ulster and Connacht one each). (Federico Meda)

'Every time they played away a horde in red would turn up to support. If you were the host club you'd love them, for the free-spending Munster fans would take over – and this was not a football crowd.'

MUNSTER ON THE MARCH

When Ross O'Carroll Kelly was conceived in 1998 and Tadhg Furlong was a six-year-old boy in short pants, Munster Rugby had yet to develop into the sporting juggernaut that would carry many thousands of fans on an odyssey around Europe. Rugby union had only turned professional in 1995 (while a more widely followed game in most countries internationally, union remained officially an amateur sport until this time, while league had turned professional by the beginning of the 20th century), and it took a year for most people in the rugby world to wake up and accept the new reality – longer still in Ireland, where the IRFU liked the old amateur ways much better than what professionalism offered.

It is unlikely the character of Ross had much traction in Limerick – the largest urban centre in Munster – when the column started up in the *Sunday Tribune*. Limerick has always had a better handle on sport for the sake of it rather than as an expression of social class. But the development of Munster as a powerhouse in European rugby was just the opportunity Munster fans needed. At the beginning of the professional era there weren't many of them – fans, that is. It was only in the season 1999/2000 that the 'Red Army' of Munster supporters mobilised and recruited and took full advantage of budget airline Ryanair's extensive network across the Continent.

When the Heineken Cup had started up in the 1995–6 season to provide a competition for players across Europe who had just turned professional and setting a new stage for the game, it had great potential but needed a storyline to develop that potential. Munster became the story.

After a few false starts they got to the 2000 final at Twickenham in London. They learned more from the defeat than they would have had they won in their first final. Northampton Saints, their opponents that day, arrived exhausted from a gruelling league schedule in England, so Munster had a clear advantage there. The night before, however, in the team room of their hotel, the Munster group met to talk about the occasion and what it meant to them. Quickly enough the meeting became heavy with emotion. Players began delivering testimonies on how much they wanted to win, for whom and why. Tears flowed. By the time the meeting broke up they had lost the advantage that should have been theirs. The game the next day was tight, and their marksman Ronan O'Gara was narrowly off target with a penalty kick that would have won it. Small margins are what count on days like that.

By the time the 2006 final rolled around Munster had been knocking on the door so hard their knuckles were raw. They were almost at a point where another defeat on a big day could do long-term damage. They had lost a semi-final, a final, another

Irish national-team kit through the years
on display at Clontarf Rugby Club, Dublin.

THE CURSE OF MAYO AND
OTHER (GAELIC) STORIES

In 1951 the team representing County
Mayo won the final of the All-Ireland Senior
Football Championship, the most important
tournament in Gaelic football, for the
second year running. Mayo is one of the
most successful teams of all time, with no
fewer than forty-eight provincial titles, but
on the all-Ireland level they have not won
since that fateful day, racking up a string
of eleven lost finals, including in 2020
and 2021. There are whispers of a curse.
Returning home from the winning match
the bus (or lorry, the details vary) carrying
the celebrating team passed in front of a
funeral, but the players failed to pause their
celebrations. The widow (or was it a priest?)
cast a hex: Mayo would never win again
until all the players in that team were dead.

Gaelic football – which, in simplified terms,
is halfway between soccer and rugby and
has many similarities with Australian rules
football – is one of the four sports overseen
by the Gaelic Athletic Association, Ireland's
largest sporting organisation, established as
part of the late-19th-century Gaelic 'revival'.
The others are Gaelic handball, hurling
(which bears some resemblance to field
hockey and which also has a women's version
called camogie) and rounders (a cousin of
baseball and softball). Collectively, they are
the most popular sports in Ireland, well ahead
of football and rugby. They are still run on
a completely amateur basis: the GAA does
not permit any form of compensation for
players or coaches. And it does not protect
them from curses either: the last surviving
player from the title-winning Mayo side of
1951, Patrick 'Paddy' Prendergast, died in
September 2021. All-Ireland, bring it on.

Scrum practice at Clontarf Rugby Club, Dublin.

THE PASSENGER Brendan Fanning

The traditional Irish women's sport is camogie, the women's variant of hurling, but rugby is becoming more popular thanks to the success of the national side, the only team to have challenged French and English dominance of the Six Nations (with title wins in 2013 and 2015). In spite of this, professional status is still a distant dream and stories like that of Linda Djougang, who played against Wales the day after a thirteen-hour hospital shift, remain the norm. And they go hand in hand with the never-ending controversy over the cavernous gulf in the way the men's and women's games are considered. This should not come as too much of a surprise, as Jill Henderson, the first Irish captain, explained in an interview for The42.ie. At the time of their international debut against Scotland in 1993, 'There were a lot of people who were against it, who were not taking us seriously. People would ask silly questions like "Is the pitch the same size? Do you have contact? Do you tackle?"' Up until 2005 none of the women players who took to the field with the shamrock on their shirts received an actual cap, unlike the men's team, and in the rugby world this is both a symbolic and a physical omission. The most recent controversy created more embarrassment than usual. Under Covid regulations, their amateur status meant that women's teams were not permitted to get changed indoors, so at the Interprovincial Championship match held at Donnybrook Stadium in Dublin the players had to change outdoors in an area near the bins. The presence of rats and social media did the rest, and the issue of gender equality was firmly back on the agenda. (Federico Meda)

two semi-finals and then a quarter-final. Every time they played away a horde in red would turn up to support. If you were the host club you'd love them, for the free-spending Munster fans would take over – and this was not a football crowd. It was a family pursuit, and there was no crowd trouble, but it brought a pressure all of its own. Supporters – drawn from across the entire community – were spending heavily to follow the team abroad, often managing to get more tickets to games than the home fans. The team needed to reward them. There had to be some payback beyond the team giving their best on the field and going close.

And in 2006 they were back in the final, this time against the French side Biarritz, who had beaten them in the quarter-final the previous season. There were 74,500 fans packed into the Millennium Stadium in Cardiff, where the roof was closed. No other Heineken Cup final had produced this sort of atmosphere; no other Heineken Cup final had produced such a lopsided contest between the fans, where Munster outnumbered the Basques ten to one. It was deafening. It was also deliverance day. The perfect illustration of how many people were on board for this journey came during a stoppage in the game when the television director cut away to a shot from O'Connell Street in Limerick city centre where a crowd of fifteen thousand were watching the match on a big screen. The same shot flashed up on screen in the stadium, so the sixty thousand-odd Munster fans in Cardiff immediately saluted the fifteen thousand back in Limerick. Biarritz, a proud club in a proud rugby region of France, hadn't a chance. It was one of the most electric moments in the history of Irish sport.

Ireland really is different.

The New Spirits of Ireland

MIRKO ZILAHY

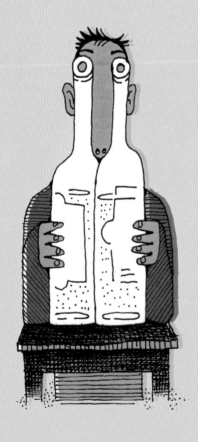

Next to the huge mirror behind the mahogany bar hangs a photograph of a man with a stocky, jovial face and a pint of stout in his hands. There are a few words at the bottom: 'I only drink on two occasions. When I'm thirsty and when I'm not.' It is signed 'Brendan Behan', the house painter, journalist, playwright and republican writer famous in his home country and the English-speaking world for his book *Borstal Boy*. We are at number 3 Henry Street, where the blue paintwork around the door and the sign adorned with a pint of Guinness welcome you to McDaids, the historic Dublin pub where Behan, a renowned stout-drinker and conversationalist, was the most famous regular.

There is no Irish writer who has not devoted a novel, essay or aphorism to the art of drinking. Even in James Joyce's *Ulysses* the protagonist Leopold Bloom wrestles with the conundrum of whether it is possible to cross Dublin without passing at least one pub. A few years ago a researcher apparently developed an algorithm that revealed a mysterious 'alcohol-free' route through the maze of the city centre, but a few days later a brand-new pub sprang up along the route, rendering the formula obsolete.

On a map of Dublin crowded with

with $1.027 billion. This revival has been driven by small businesses that share a desire to reclaim tradition and reinvent products in tune with modern times and modern tastes. A case in point is the Tipperary Boutique Distillery, founded in 2014, which is following up on its extremely popular vintage Single Grain by releasing its first Single Estate Irish Single Malt, the ultimate expression of the 'spirit' of the terroir, made with raw materials originating from its own Ballindoney Farm in the wonderful Tipperary countryside. Much further west, the Dingle Distillery opened in 2012, creating extremely high-quality gin and vodka. Since 2016 it has produced an excellent single malt, triple-distilled in accordance with the Irish tradition. Following a similar path, after conquering the international market with its Gunpowder Irish Gin, the Shed Distillery (2014) developed Drumshanbo, named after the village where it is based on Lough Allen in County Leitrim. It is a single pot still whiskey – which is made with both malted and unmalted barley – and, as such, the first to be produced in Connacht, Ireland's wild west, for over a century. But perhaps the most ambitious brand on the scene is Teeling (2015), the first new distillery to open in Dublin recently, a stone's throw from St Patrick's Cathedral. Teeling has devoted itself to unconventional distilling techniques, creating unique and highly sought-after brands such as Teeling Single Grain (with 95 per cent maize), Teeling Single Malt (barley malt distilled and aged in five different types of cask) and Teeling Small Batch, a blend of grain and malt whiskey aged in bourbon and rum casks. With artisan distilleries popping up like mushrooms all across the country, updating the map of the new wave of Irish whiskey will take more than just an algorithm.

drinking establishments you will find the Golden Triangle, the area closely associated with the spirit of the Emerald Isle: *uisce beatha*, the 'water of life', the Irish Gaelic for whiskey (note: whiskey with an 'e' unlike Scotch whisky). For four hundred years – at least since King James I of England and Ireland (James VI of Scotland) granted a licence to distil to Sir Thomas Phillips, the landowner in Bushmills, County Antrim – the water of life was distributed all around the world, and for centuries Ireland's historic rivals in Scotland had to make do with second place in the global rankings. This was, however, disrupted when production collapsed in the early 20th century during the Irish War of Independence and Civil War as well as fallout from the effects of Prohibition in the United States, which wiped out a large part of the market. As late as the 1970s only two big brands remained on the island, the New Midleton Distillery and the Old Bushmills Distillery.

But the Celtic Tiger has accustomed us to its stunning feats of agility, and since the 2010s we have witnessed a genuine renaissance in Irish whiskey, to the extent that 2020 saw Ireland become the world's third largest exporter of whisk(e)y, with sales worth $778 million, after Great Britain with $5.015 billion and the USA

An Author Recommends

A book, a film and
an album to understand
Ireland, chosen by:

LISA MCINERNEY

The Irish writer and blogger Lisa McInerney
achieved fame with her blog 'Arse End of
Ireland', in which she recounted, under the
pseudonym Sweary Lady, life in social housing
in the city of Galway. Her first novel was 2015's
The Glorious Heresies (Crown, USA/John
Murray, UK), winner of the Women's Prize for
Fiction and the Desmond Elliott Prize in 2016,
and she has published two other novels with
John Murray, *The Blood Miracles* (2018) and
The Rules of Revelation (2021).

THE BOOK

NIGHT BOAT TO TANGIER
Kevin Barry
Doubleday, 2019 (USA)
/ Canongate, 2019 (UK)

Charlie and Maurice are aging Corkonian
gangsters waiting at the port of Algeciras
for the boat to come in from Tangier,
on which Maurice's estranged daughter
Dilly might be travelling. They reminisce,
debate, joke and judge while grief, regret
and resentment churn under every word
and action. It is a testament to the magic
of translation that the peculiar way Irish
people talk at, rather than to, one another
might be understood in another language:
Night Boat, like all of Kevin Barry's work,
is unapologetically Irish. Barry celebrates
the shiftiness of Irish vernacular, knows
instinctively how much is left unspoken
or alluded to, wields our kind of vague
dishonesty fearlessly, puts it to work.
Where some Irish authors might baulk
at using the peculiarities of Hiberno-
English – the layered slang and knotty
syntax left over from Gaeilge – or acqui-
esce to overseas editors' doubts, Barry
gets mischievous and defiant. And this
is just the raw material of *Night Boat*. In
the macro, it tackles themes of social
class, gender, friendship and love – more
than anything else, love. I endorsed this
book on publication and said of it that
it was Kevin Barry at his most tender,
and that remains true. Not just love of
the Hiberno-English dialect but love for
the Irish landscape and its verbose, slippery, bruised, sentimental people surges
through this novel.

THE FILM

THE COMMITMENTS
Alan Parker
1991

It's strange to think that *The Commitments* doesn't qualify as a contemporary film any more, it being thirty years old. Thirty! I can scarcely believe it, because it feels contemporary, even though it was made at a time when Ireland was still staunchly Catholic, under-resourced and under-funded, its ordinary people detached from their own cultural heritage. Here's the thing: *The Commitments* helped change that, at least in my head, and I was too young to see it when it was released, which adds to my conviction that it's almost timeless. Here we were, finally in the spotlight, the urban working class of Ireland, vibrant and rebellious and proud against what I suppose you might have called squalor. Here were people I recognised: profane, cheeky, morally inconsistent and endlessly creative. Adapted from Roddy Doyle's breakneck novel, the film follows Jimmy Rabbitte Jr, a roguish Dubliner with a love of soul music and a determination to bring it to his beleaguered compatriots. Although directed by an Englishman (imagine!), it's a film that understands the Irish condition, our perpetual anxiety about being outside of things, inferior and insecure; when saxophonist Dean suggests that the band is 'maybe a little white' to perform soul music, Jimmy, fiercely attesting to solidarity between oppressed peoples, entreats the band to proclaim, 'I'm black, and I'm proud.' He doesn't succeed in this or in his broader mission, which is the only authentic result, one Beckett himself would approve of. 'Ever tried. Ever failed. No matter. Try again. Fail again. Fail better.'

THE ALBUM

THE ART OF PRETENDING TO SWIM
Villagers
2018

For many outside of Ireland, Irish music means traditional music – fiddles, bodhráns, tin whistles – or perhaps the stadium rock of 1980s-era U2. But Irish music is as much about lyrical innovation; the same wordplay, self-contemplation and emotional spill that is championed in our best literature. Villagers, founded and fronted by Dún Laoghaire native Conor O'Brien, typifies this approach to storytelling through music. The expansive sound of *The Art of Pretending to Swim* suits its big questions about identity, love, faith, contentment in a world illuminated by smartphone screens; big questions asked circuitously and left unanswered. Irish people are preoccupied with big questions, particularly about Irishness. This country changed almost incomprehensibly in the space of a generation, from poor and pious and resigned to perpetual emigration, to secular, liberal and wealthy, so perhaps it should not surprise an onlooker that we so enjoy defining and then redefining. As does O'Brien, who has turned his back on Ireland, returned to Ireland, rejected faith, reimagined faith. It might be said of *The Art of Pretending to Swim* that it doesn't sound particularly Irish – and for 'particularly' we might substitute 'self-consciously' – but to an Irish ear it is unmistakably Irish, pushing for the profound despite the risks in wearing one's heart on one's sleeve ... arch disingenuity and dry detachment be damned! 'My heart is spilling over/crashing on the ground' sings O'Brien on 'A Trick of the Light'. Ours with him.

The Playlist

You can listen to this playlist at:
open.spotify.com/user/iperborea

KEIRAN GODDARD

It's always a strange thing to try to sum up or capture what the music of a particular place sounds like. Like trying to pin down a cloud. It would be easy to tie myself in knots, trying to span all of the things that strike me as important: the politics, the shifting demographics, conflicts historical and present, the points where traditional sounds creep in and the fissures where those sounds are actively discarded or challenged.

So, to keep it simple, I have just chosen twelve songs that I love. And luckily, thankfully, as is often the way with such things, the heart and the ear are one step ahead of the brain anyway. Denise Chaila is unreal, all bounce and wit and fearlessness; a black African-Irish artist rapping about identity and heritage and bell hooks and philosophy and making you want to dance like a lunatic in the process.

There are nods to the much-maligned singer-songwriter tradition with the Villagers and Damian Dempsey, proving that in the right hands it's still a mode that can be genuinely affecting. Likewise, Two Door Cinema Club show that if your song is good enough it can be used on as many adverts as you like and still sound absolutely amazing.

Tebi Rex and Bicep are perhaps the most emblematic artists in the list. Hard to pin down, a deeply exciting mix of hip-hop, jazz and electronica that feels both familiar and, in the best possible sense, disorientating. And a final shout out has to go to CMAT for her brilliant doo-wop-inspired track. After all, if you haven't considered weeping in a KFC at least once in your life, then I'm afraid we can't be friends ...

1

Denise Chaila
Copper Bullet
2019

2

The Frames
Red Chord
1996

3

God Knows
Who's Asking?
2020

4

Bicep, Four Tet
Opal
2018

5

Villagers
*A Trick of the
Light*
2018

6

Hozier
*Take Me
to Church*
2013

7

Girl Band
In Plastic
2015

8

CMAT
*Another Day
(kfc)*
2020

9

Tebi Rex,
Local Boy
*I Never Got Off
the Bus*
2019

10

Damien Dempsey,
the Dubliners
*A Rainy Night
in Soho*
2008

11

Two Door
Cinema Club
What You Know
2010

12

Sinéad O'Connor
*He Moved
Through the Fair*
1997

Digging Deeper

FICTION

Sara Baume
Spill Simmer Falter Wither
Tramp Press, 2015 (Ireland) / Mariner, 2016 (USA) / Windmill, 2018 (UK)

Claire-Louise Bennett
Pond
Stinging Fly, 2015 (Ireland) / Riverhead, 2017 (USA) / Fitzcarraldo, 2015 (UK)

Anna Burns
Milkman
Graywolf, 2018 (USA) / Faber and Faber, 2018 (UK)

Roddy Doyle
Smile
Viking, 2017 (USA) / Vintage, 2018 (UK)

Anne Enright
The Green Road
W.W. Norton, 2016 (USA) / Vintage, 2016 (UK)

Sinéad Gleeson (ed.)
The Long Gaze Back: An Anthology of Irish Women Writers
New Island Books, 2016

Paul Lynch
Red Sky in Morning
Black Bay, 2014 (USA) / Quercus, 2014 (UK)

Eimear McBride
A Girl Is a Half-Formed Thing
Hogarth, 2015 (USA) / Faber and Faber, 2014 (UK)

Lisa McInerney
The Glorious Heresies
Crown, 2016 (USA) / John Murray, 2015 (UK)

Paul Murray
Skippy Dies
Farrar, Straus and Giroux, 2011 (USA) / Penguin, 2011 (UK)

Sally Rooney
Normal People
Hogarth, 2020 (USA) / Faber and Faber, 2019 (UK)

Colm Tóibín
Nora Webster
Scribner, 2015 (USA) / Penguin, 2015 (UK)

NON-FICTION

Catherine Dunne
An Unconsidered People: The Irish in London
New Island Books, 2021 (rev. ed.)

Caelainn Hogan
Republic of Shame: How Ireland Punished 'Fallen Women' and Their Children
Penguin, 2020

Ed Moloney
The Secret History of the IRA
W.W. Norton, 2003 (USA) / Penguin, 2007 (UK)

Patrick Radden Keefe
Say Nothing: A True Story of Murder and Memory in Northern Ireland
Doubleday, 2019 (USA) / William Collins, 2019 (UK)

Alison O'Reilly
*My Name Is Bridget: The Untold
Story of Bridget Dolan and the
Tuam Mother and Baby Home*
Gill Books, 2018

Fintan O'Toole
*We Don't Know Ourselves: A Personal
History of Modern Ireland*
Liveright, 2022 (USA) /
Head of Zeus, 2021 (UK)

Emilie Pine
Notes to Self
Tramp Press, 2018 (Ireland) / Dial Press,
2019 (USA) / Penguin, 2019 (UK)

Melatu Uche Okorie
*This Hostel Life: Stories of Migrant
Women in a Hidden Ireland*
Skein Press, 2018 (Ireland) /
Virago, 2019 (USA, UK)

Kerri ní Dochartaigh
Thin Places
Canongate, 2021

Ian Cobain
*Anatomy of a Killing: Life and
Death on a Divided Island*
Granta, 2021

Charles Townshend
The Partition: Ireland Divided, 1885–1925
Allen Lane, 2021

Robert L. Harris
*Returning Light: 30 Years of
Life on Skellig Michael*
HarperCollins Ireland, 2021

Susan McKay
*Northern Protestants:
On Shifting Ground*
Blackstaff Press, 2021

FILM, TV AND DOCUMENTARIES

Lenny Abrahamson
What Richard Did
2012

Yann Demange
'71
2014

Stephen Frears
Philomena
2013

Steve Humphries
Sex in a Cold Climate
1998

Aideen Kane, Maeve O'Boyle
and Lucy Kennedy
The 8th
2021

Lisa McGee
Derry Girls
2018–

Graham Linehan and Arthur Mathews
Father Ted
1995–8

Peter Mullan
Magdalene
2002

Graphic design and art direction: Tomo Tomo
and Pietro Buffa
Photography: Kenneth O Halloran
Photographic content curated by Prospekt Photographers
Illustrations: Edoardo Massa
Infographics and cartography: Pietro Buffa

Managing editor (English-language edition): Simon Smith

Thanks to: Ada Arduini, Simon Carswell, Catherine Dunne,
Catherine Eccles, Gerry Edwards, Alessandro Foggetta,
Keiran Goddard, Sinéad Mac Aodha and Literature Ireland,
Marinella Magrì, Federico Meda, Valentina Salaris,
Dario Scovacricchi, Martyn Turner

http://europaeditions.com/thepassenger
http://europaeditions.co.uk/thepassenger
#ThePassengerMag

The Passenger – Ireland
© Iperborea S.r.l., Milan, and Europa Editions, 2022

Translations from the Italian: Alan Thawley
Translations © Iperborea S.r.l., Milan, and Europa Editions,
2022

ISBN 9781787703780

Printed on Munken Pure thanks to the support
of Arctic Paper

Printed by ELCOGRAF S.p.A., Verona, Italy

People